Instagram Marketing

The Best Tips & Tricks to Grow Your Business

(Tips and Tricks for Better Conversions Using Instagram Marketing Strategies)

David Batson

Published By **John Kembrey**

David Batson

Instagram Marketing: The Best Tips & Tricks to Grow Your Business (Tips and Tricks for Better Conversions Using Instagram Marketing Strategies)

ISBN   978-1-7775102-9-9

Legal & Disclaimer

The information contained in this book is not designed to replace or take the place of any form of medicine or professional medical advice. The information in this book has been provided for educational & entertainment purposes only.

The information contained in this book has been compiled from sources deemed reliable, and it is accurate to the best of the Author's knowledge; however, the Author cannot guarantee its accuracy and validity and cannot be held liable for any errors or omissions. Changes are periodically made to this book. You must consult your doctor or get professional medical advice before using any of the suggested remedies, techniques, or information in this book.

Table Of Contents

Chapter 1: Setting up Your Instagram Business Account

Creating an Instagram business enterprise account is the first step towards harnessing the platform's advertising and advertising capability. Here's a look at to guide you thru the system:

Why Choose a Business Account?

A industrial organisation account offers treasured competencies and insights that are not available with private payments.

It allows you to function contact facts, making it less complex for clients to acquire you.

Access to Instagram Insights offers crucial statistics about your target audience and content material ordinary universal performance.

Steps to Set Up Your Business Account:

1. Log In or Sign Up: If you already have a personal Instagram account, you can convert

it to a business account. If now not, down load the Instagram app and be a part of up together along with your e mail or phone massive variety.

2. Profile Setup: Once logged in, navigate to your profile via tapping your profile photograph in the bottom proper. Tap the 3 horizontal strains within the top right nook and then faucet "Settings." Scroll down and pick "Switch to Professional Account."

3. Choose a Category: Select the magnificence that outstanding represents your business. This permits Instagram understand your location of interest and advise your content material material material to applicable customers.

4. Connect to Facebook: Linking your Instagram account to a Facebook Page is vital for having access to more business enterprise abilties and taking walks commercials. If you do now not have a Facebook Page, create one.

5. Complete Your Profile: Add vital records like your business enterprise's call, profile image (e.G., brand), and speak to records (email, cellular telephone quantity, deal with).

6. Enhance Your Bio: Craft a concise and engaging bio that highlights what your agency offers and why clients need to examine you. Include applicable key phrases.

7. Contact Options: Make sure to allow contact options along with e mail, smartphone, or guidelines simply so clients can without troubles obtain you.

eight. Done! Congratulations, you currently have a completely practical Instagram company account.

Benefits of a Business Account:

Instagram Insights: Gain get entry to to target audience demographics, placed up basic overall performance, and insights into your lovers' conduct.

Promotions: Run paid promotions proper now out of your account to reap a broader target audience.

Contact Information: Display your e mail, telephone sizable variety, and address for easy patron touch.

Shopping: If you're an e-exchange employer, you may permit Instagram Shopping to tag products in your posts.

By installing place your Instagram enterprise corporation account, you loose up treasured tools and facts to help you tailor your content material and method to higher connect with your target market and gather your advertising and advertising and marketing dreams. It's a essential step for your adventure in the direction of Instagram advertising and advertising success.

2.1 Creating a Business Pro le on Instagram

Creating a enterprise profile on Instagram is a pivotal step on social media marketing and advertising journey. It offers various blessings and gadget that empower you to efficiently promote your logo, products, or services. Here's the way to create a business organization profile:

Step 1: Existing or New Account

If you've got already got a private Instagram account that you want to convert into a business employer profile, log in. If not, down load the Instagram app and sign on the use of your email address or cellphone range.

Step 2: Access Profile Settings

Once you are logged in, tap to your profile image in the backside proper corner to get right of access on your profile.

In the pinnacle-proper nook of your profile, tap the three horizontal traces to open the menu.

Tap "Settings" at the bottom of the menu. Step 3: Switch to Professional Account

Under "Settings," scroll down and faucet "Account."

5

Then, tap "Switch to Professional Account."

Step 4: Choose Your Business Category

Instagram will activate you to pick out out a category that exceptional represents your enterprise. This enables Instagram understand your niche and advise your content to the right target marketplace.

You can always alternate or update this beauty later if preferred.

Step five: Connect to a Facebook Page

If you have were given a Facebook Page in your industrial organization, connect it on your Instagram account. This step gives get right of entry to to more enterprise functions and the functionality to run advertisements.

If you do not have a Facebook Page, you may create one immediately from the Instagram app.

Step 6: Fill in Your Business Details

Instagram will ask for essential industrial business enterprise facts, together with your commercial agency's call, profile photo (e.G., your emblem), and call info together with an electronic mail deal with, cellphone huge variety, and bodily deal with (if applicable).

Ensure that your commercial commercial enterprise employer facts are correct and updated.

Step 7: Review and Finish

Review your company profile facts to make certain the entirety is correct.

Once you are satisfied, tap "Done."

Congratulations! You now have a commercial enterprise business enterprise profile on Instagram.

With your commercial enterprise profile, you can free up a fixed of equipment and capabilities, on the side of Instagram Insights for tracking your common performance, the capability to run promotions, and get right of entry to to contact options that make it a whole lot less tough for clients to gain you. It's a critical step in organising your brand's on line presence and appealing along facet your audience efficiently.

2.2 To link your Instagram commercial agency account to a Facebook Page,

Step 1: Ensure You're an Admin

Make great you have got admin get right of entry to to the Facebook Page you want to link in your Instagram account.

Step 2: Open Instagram

Open the Instagram app in your cell tool.

Step 3: Go to Your Profile

Tap to your profile photo or icon within the bottom right nook to get right of entry to your profile.

Step four: Access Settings

In your profile, tap the 3 horizontal strains within the pinnacle-right corner to open the menu.

Step five: Open Account Settings

Scroll down and faucet "Settings" at the lowest of the menu.

Step 6: Link to Facebook

Under "Settings," tap "Account."

Step 7: Connect to Facebook

In the "Account" phase, faucet "Linked Accounts."

Step eight: Choose Facebook

Tap "Facebook" to attach your Instagram account to your Facebook Page.

Step 9: Log in to Facebook

You'll be added approximately to log in to your Facebook account in case you are not already logged in.

Step 10: Select the Page

After logging in, Instagram will display a list of Facebook Pages that you manage or have get admission to to.

Select the Facebook Page you want to hyperlink to your Instagram account.

Step 11: Confirm Settings

Instagram will ask for permissions to manipulate your Page and profile, in addition to to perform responsibilities which includes developing and managing commercials. Confirm these permissions.

Step 12: Finish Linking

Once you've showed the permissions, your Instagram employer account will be associated with your chosen Facebook Page. =Note: If you do no longer see your Facebook Page indexed, make certain you are an admin of the Page and that you've logged in with the proper Facebook account.

Congratulations, your Instagram commercial company account is now connected on your

Facebook Page. This connection lets in you to get admission to more agency skills, run advertisements, and pass-sell content material efficaciously on each systems.

2.Three Choosing a Pro le Picture and Crafting an E ective Bio on Instagram

Your Instagram profile photograph and bio are important factors that make a long-lasting first affect on visitors. Here's the way to purpose them to rely:

Profile Picture:

Your profile photograph is the scene example of your emblem. For organizations, this is usually a logo, while human beings may additionally use a professional headshot.

Ensure your profile image is apparent, exquisite, and straight away recognizable, despite the reality that appeared as a small thumbnail.

The encouraged profile photo duration is 110 x a hundred and ten pixels, and it is displayed as a circle. So, ensure your photo fits nicely internal this spherical body.

Regularly update your profile picture to align with contemporary branding or promotions. Bio:

Your bio is your opportunity to offer a picture of your brand's identification and what internet site traffic can count on out of your Instagram account.

Chapter 2: Developing an E Active Content Strategy for Instagram

A nicely-defined content material cloth method is crucial for attractive your goal marketplace, building logo identification, and challenge your advertising and marketing desires on Instagram. Here's a entire manual:

1. Define Your Goals:

Start with the useful resource of figuring out your dreams. Are you aiming to increase emblem hobby, power net website online website visitors, enhance income, or sell a particular advertising campaign? Your dreams will shape your content material technique.

2. Know Your Audience:

Understanding your target marketplace is important. Conduct studies to decide their demographics, pastimes, ache factors, and conduct on Instagram.

three. Develop a Unique Brand Voice and Aesthetic:

Your emblem voice must align along with your logo's personality. Are you informal, expert, witty, or inspirational? Ensure consistency across all of your content material.

Create a visible aesthetic that suggests your emblem's identity. Consider coloration schemes, filters, and subjects that resonate collectively along side your target market.

4. Content Calendar and Planning:

Create a content material cloth material calendar to prepare your posts. Plan earlier to hold consistency and make sure that your content fabric material aligns collectively together with your dreams.

Balance your content material fabric fabric aggregate. Include an entire lot of publish sorts, together with product photographs, in the back of-the-scenes glimpses, consumer-generated content, and extra.

5. Types of Posts:

Photos: Showcase your merchandise, offerings, or emblem way of existence with notable snap shots.

Videos: Capture interest with quick, attractive video content material. Consider tutorials, demonstrations, or storytelling.

Stories: Share ephemeral content material cloth like promotions, sneak peeks, and interactive polls.

IGTV: Explore longer-shape video content fabric for in-depth storytelling or tutorials.

Live: Connect together together together with your target marketplace in actual-time thru net hosting live Q&A classes, product launches, or tutorials.

6. Content Themes and Series:

Develop habitual content subjects or series that your target market can appearance beforehand to. For example, "Throwback Thursdays" or "Product Spotlight Tuesdays."

7. Use Instagram Features:

Leverage Instagram's features, on the aspect of carousels, shoppable posts, and stickers like polls, questions, and quizzes in Stories. 8. Tell Stories:

Share compelling logo reminiscences that resonate collectively along with your target audience. Stories help construct emotional connections and engagement.

nine. User-Generated Content (UGC):

Encourage your customers to create content material providing your products or services. Repost UGC to build take delivery of as proper with and show off client satisfaction.

10. Consistency is Key:

Maintain a regular posting time table. Consistency continues your goal market engaged and informed.

11. Engagement and Interaction:

Respond to feedback, interact together collectively along with your target market via likes and remarks on their posts, and foster a experience of community.

12. Data-Driven Decision Making:

Regularly study your content cloth's performance using Instagram Insights. Adjust your approach based totally on what works exceptional for your target audience.

thirteen. Stay Trendy and Relevant:

Participate in well-known challenges, trends, and hashtags at the same time as relevant to your brand. 14. Collaboration and Partnerships:

Collaborate with influencers or complementary producers to extend your reap and credibility.

15. Call-to-Action (CTA):

Include a CTA to your posts. Encourage customers to take precise actions, inclusive of travelling your net internet web page, following your account, or growing a purchase.

16. Monitor Competitors:

Keep a watch fixed on your competition' content fabric and engagement strategies to end up aware about opportunities and stay in advance.

A nicely-achieved content cloth technique on Instagram can help you bring together a dedicated following, energy conversions, and obtain your business enterprise targets. Continuously test and refine your approach to conform to converting dispositions and target marketplace alternatives.

three.1 De ning Your Brand Voice and Aesthetic on Instagram

Your brand's voice and aesthetic on Instagram are key factors that help your content cloth stand out and connect with your target audience. Here's the way to outline them successfully:

Brand Voice:

1. Understand Your Brand Personality:

Consider your emblem's values, mission, and person. Are you formal or casual, severe or playful, expert or informal? Define the tone that aligns together collectively with your emblem. 2. Know Your Audience:

Understand your goal market's options and conversation fashion. Your emblem voice need to resonate with them. 3. Create Brand Guidelines:

Develop clean logo pointers that outline your logo's voice, alongside facet the use of language, tone, and key messaging. Four. Consistency is Key:

Maintain consistency to your logo voice at some point of all content material material and interactions on Instagram.

five. Use Stories and Emotion:

Storytelling can be a effective manner to

deliver your brand's message and values.

Create narratives that evoke emotion and

resonate in conjunction with your goal marketplace.

6. Engage Authentically:

Be actual and real for your

interactions with fans. Respond to

comments and messages in a ordinary and

personable manner.

Brand Aesthetic:

1. Color Palette:

Choose a coloration palette that represents your emblem. Use those hues constantly in your posts, stories, and everyday profile. 2. Visual Style:

Define the seen fashion of your content material fabric. Are you the use of immoderate-assessment pictures, muted tones, excellent and colourful visuals, or a few element else?

three. Filters and Editing:

If you operate filters or picture improving, stay with

a particular style or set of presets to preserve a

cohesive appearance.

four. Consistent Imagery:

Maintain a everyday fashion within the shape of

imagery you operate. This need to encompass product

photos, manner of lifestyles snap shots, or patron-generated

content material fabric.

5. Grid Layout:

Plan your grid format to make certain that the

regular look of your profile is visually

attractive. Consider the usage of alternating

content material types or colour styles.

6. Branded Elements:

Incorporate branded elements together with logos, watermarks, or overlays on the identical time as relevant.

7. Story Highlights:

Organize your Instagram Stories

Highlights with cohesive cover pix and

thematic groupings.

eight. Experiment and Evolve:

While consistency is essential, it's also

good enough to test and evolve your

aesthetic as your logo grows and modifications.

Examples:

If you are a health brand, your emblem voice might be motivational and enthusiastic. Your aesthetic have to include colourful, immoderate-power photographs with shiny colours.

For a steeply-priced style logo, your voice might be contemporary-day and aspirational. Your aesthetic might also moreover want to involve the usage of elegant, terrific imagery with a sophisticated colour palette.

Remember that your emblem voice and aesthetic need to authentically constitute your emblem and resonate along with your target market. Regularly have a study how well your voice and aesthetic align in conjunction with your logo's goals and make adjustments as desired.

three.2 Creating a Content Calendar and Planning Your Instagram Posts

An prepared content material calendar is essential for keeping a steady and effective Instagram presence. Here's the way to create one and plan your posts:

1. Set Clear Goals:

Define your Instagram advertising and advertising desires, whether or not or not it is developing brand focus, using internet website online site visitors, or boosting income.

2. Know Your Audience:

Understand your goal marketplace's opportunities, behaviors, and top engagement times on Instagram.

three. Choose Posting Frequency:

Decide how frequently you could submit. Consistency is fundamental, but first rate want to never be sacrificed for quantity.

4. Create a Calendar:

Use a digital calendar or a spreadsheet to devise your Instagram content material material. Many social media manipulate equipment moreover provide content scheduling abilities.

5. Theme and Content Mix:

Determine the content problem subjects and brands you want to encompass in your calendar. This should consist of product showcases, behind-the-scenes glimpses, consumer-generated content material material, and further.

6. Plan Ahead:

Plan content material material at the least a few weeks in advance. This lets in for better steerage and coordination.

7. Include Special Occasions:

Factor in vacations, activities, product launches, and campaigns which might be relevant for your brand.

eight. Content Variations:

Ensure a numerous mixture of content cloth, which include pics, movies, Stories, and IGTV. Mix promotional posts with attractive and informative content material.

nine. Hashtags and Captions:

Plan hashtags and write captions in advance. Ensure that they align collectively together

together with your content material cloth and emblem voice.

10. Content Creation:

Allocate time for content cloth advent, which consist of pics, video production, and layout artwork. Ensure that content material fabric fabric meets best requirements.

eleven. Scheduling:

Use scheduling gadget to devise and automate posts. Schedule content material for peak engagement times primarily based surely for your target market's conduct.

12. Engagement Strategy:

Plan time for attractive together together with your target audience with the resource of responding to remarks, likes, and messages.

thirteen. Review and Adjust:

Regularly examine your content material fabric calendar to evaluate what is strolling and what dreams improvement. Be bendy and prepared to alter your plan based totally on average overall performance information. Tools for Content Planning:

Social media manage equipment like Buffer, Hootsuite, and Later allow you to time table and manipulate your Instagram posts correctly.

Content advent tool like Canva and Adobe Spark assist in designing enticing visuals.

Example Calendar:

Monday: Product display off

Tuesday: User-generated content fabric feature

Chapter 3: Hash Tags and Discovery on Instagram

Using hashtags strategically is a powerful manner to growth the discoverability of your Instagram posts and achieve a broader target marketplace. Here's the way to make the most of hashtags:

1. Choose Relevant Hashtags:

Research and select out hashtags which may be

right now associated with your content material material, brand, and

target market. Aim for a combination of massive and

place of interest-particular hashtags.

2. Avoid Overused Hashtags:

While famous hashtags can increase

visibility, they'll be also quite aggressive.

Consider the use of a combination of much less

aggressive, prolonged-tail hashtags to improve

your probabilities of being seen.

3. Create Your Branded Hashtag:

Develop a completely unique, branded hashtag that represents your emblem or advertising marketing campaign.

Encourage enthusiasts to apply it even as sharing content cloth related to your logo.

four. Use Location-Based Hashtags:

Include vicinity-based completely hashtags to draw

close by audiences in case your commercial enterprise employer serves a

specific geographic location.

five. Research Hashtag Trends:

Stay up to date on trending and seasonal

hashtags. Participate in relevant developments to

improve visibility.

6. Limit the Number of Hashtags:

While Instagram permits up to 30

hashtags consistent with located up, it's far high-quality to interest on

outstanding over quantity. Aim for a mixture of five to

15 pretty relevant hashtags.

7. Include Hashtags in Captions and

Comments:

You can consist of hashtags to your placed up captions or as a separate remark. Both techniques are effective, so pick what fits your aesthetic.

eight. Test Hashtags:

Regularly study your hashtag

usual overall performance to look which of them electricity the maximum engagement and discoverability.

Adjust your hashtag technique consequently.

9. Monitor Hashtag Insights:

Instagram Insights gives statistics on how

nicely your posts perform with specific

hashtags. Use this records to refine your

hashtag method.

10. Encourage User Engagement:

Encourage fans to interact with

your hashtags with the useful aid of internet
website hosting contests,

traumatic conditions, or asking for their input
in

captions.

11. Avoid Banned or Restricted Hashtags:

Be cautious approximately the use of
hashtags that

had been banned or confined thru Instagram.

Using these can negatively effect your

placed up's visibility.

12. Mix Up Hashtag Types:

Use a combination of numerous hashtag
sorts,

which incorporates enterprise-specific,
trending, and

network hashtags, to diversify your

acquire.

13. Research Competitors:

Check out what hashtags your

competition are using correctly. This can

provide insights into effective hashtags for

your niche.

14. Hashtags in Stories and Bio:

Don't forget about to apply hashtags in your

Instagram Stories and bio. Stories with hashtags have a chance to seem within the Explore web page's hashtag Stories.

15. Analyze and Adapt:

Regularly assessment your hashtag method, tune everyday overall performance, and adapt to adjustments for your content fabric fabric or industry developments.

Using hashtags effectively can notably enhance your posts' discoverability and help you hook up with a broader purpose market on Instagram. It's an critical part of building an engaged network round your logo.

four.1 Using Relevant Hashtags E ectively on Instagram

Using applicable hashtags on Instagram can substantially enhance the discoverability of your content fabric and be a part of you alongside aspect your goal market. Here's a way to apply them effectively:

1. Research and Understand Your Audience:

To use relevant hashtags, you want to understand your target market's hobbies, behaviors, and the hashtags they agree to. Research their alternatives thoroughly. 2. Choose Specific and Niche-Related Hashtags:

Use hashtags which might be straight away associated with your content fabric fabric or area of hobby. Specific and niche-related hashtags are much more likely to draw an engaged target market.

3. Mix Up Hashtag Types:

Include loads of hashtag types on your

posts, which encompass business enterprise-specific, trending, and community hashtags. This diversifies your attain.

four. Include Location-Based Hashtags:

If your content fabric is area-particular, encompass applicable region-based totally completely hashtags to aim community audiences.

five. Check Hashtag Popularity:

Evaluate the recognition of hashtags using

device like Instagram's are looking for characteristic or

1/3-celebration hashtag analytics gear. Use a

blend of famous and much less aggressive ones.

6. Create Branded Hashtags:

Develop precise branded hashtags that

constitute your emblem or campaigns.

Encourage your goal market to apply them at the same time as

posting content material material related to your logo.

7. Limit the Number of Hashtags:

Instagram allows as much as 30 hashtags in keeping with

positioned up, but it is great to interest on brilliant over amount. Aim for spherical five to 15 in particular relevant hashtags.

8. Use Hashtags in Captions and Comments:

You can region hashtags to your placed up captions or as a separate declaration. Both strategies are powerful, so pick out out out what fits your submit's aesthetic.

nine. Test and Monitor Performance:

Regularly take a look at superb hashtags and display their performance the use of Instagram Insights. Identify which ones pressure the maximum engagement and reap.

10. Avoid Banned or Restricted Hashtags:

Be cautious about the usage of hashtags that have been banned or restrained with the useful resource of Instagram. Using the ones can negatively effect your publish's visibility.

eleven. Be Specific and Descriptive:

Use descriptive and clean hashtags that

immediately relate to the content material material fabric on your positioned up.

Avoid indistinct or unrelated tags.

12. Include Relevant Hashtags in Stories

and Bio:

Don't forget about approximately to apply relevant hashtags in

your Instagram Stories and bio. Stories with

hashtags have a threat to appear in the

Explore internet internet page's hashtag Stories.

13. Encourage User Engagement:

Encourage your fans to engage

collectively with your hashtags via hosting contests,

stressful conditions, or soliciting for their critiques in

captions.

14. Research Competitors:

Analyze what hashtags your opposition

are using correctly. This can provide insights into powerful hashtags for your area of hobby.

15. Regularly Update Your Hashtag Strategy:

Instagram tendencies and purchaser behavior trade through the years. Regularly replace and adapt your hashtag approach to live relevant and effective.

Using relevant hashtags is a important hassle of Instagram advertising. When performed correctly, it could growth your content material material's achieve, engagement, and visibility amongst your purpose market.

4.2 Researching Trending Hashtags on Instagram

Keeping up with trending hashtags on Instagram can assist beautify the visibility of your content cloth and have interaction with a broader target market. Here's how to analyze and use trending hashtags efficiently:

1. Explore the Instagram Explore Page:

Instagram's Explore net web page frequently talents

trending and popular content material. Check it

regularly to find out relevant hashtags and

dispositions.

2. Use Instagram's Search Function:

Type key terms or terms associated with your

area of hobby or content material cloth into Instagram's searching for bar.

Instagram will recommend related hashtags,

some of which may be trending.

three. Explore "Top" and "Recent" Posts:

When you search for a specific hashtag,

you could see every "Top" and "Recent" tabs. "Top" posts encompass the maximum well-known and attractive content material using that hashtag. "Recent" posts display the cutting-edge content material fabric.

four. Follow Influential Accounts:

Influential bills in your area of interest regularly

use trending hashtags. Follow the ones bills

to live updated on cutting-edge-day-day tendencies.

five. Use Hashtag Analytics Tools:

There are numerous 1/3-birthday celebration device and

apps that offer insights into trending

hashtags. These equipment can help you find out

what's presently famous and applicable on your

place of interest.

6. Check Trending Events and Seasons:

Pay interest to trendy-day events, holidays,

and seasons. Create content fabric that relates to

those events and use relevant trending

hashtags.

7. Participate in Challenges:

Instagram stressful conditions frequently encompass precise hashtags. Participating in the ones challenges can raise your content material's

visibility.

eight. Monitor Competitors:

Keep an eye fixed constant on what hashtags your opposition are using. While you shouldn't duplicate their technique, it may offer insights into trending tags in your niche.

nine. Be Timely and Relevance:

Timing is important while using trending

hashtags. Make fantastic your content is relevant

to the fashion, and submit on the right moment to

maximize its effect.

10. Create Content Around Trends:

Craft content material that aligns with trending

hashtags and gives price to your

target audience. Don't pressure your content material material into

traits if it does no longer healthful glaringly.

11. Engage with Trending Content:

Engage with trending content material fabric cloth through liking,

commenting, and sharing posts that use the

trending hashtags. This permit you to get

observed thru a miles wider goal market.

12. Track Performance:

Use Instagram Insights to track how

properly your posts carry out when using trending

hashtags. Adjust your method primarily based totally totally on

what works satisfactory in your goal market.

Remember that even as the usage of trending

hashtags can decorate your content material fabric's visibility,

it's far essential to hold authenticity and

relevance on your emblem. Don't use trending

hashtags totally for the sake of it; make sure they

align collectively along with your content material and target market.

4.Three Understanding the Instagram Explore Page

The Instagram Explore Page is a outstanding characteristic of the platform designed to help customers find out new content material and debts that align with their interests. It's a precious device for each clients and agencies trying to growth their visibility and engagement. Here's the way it really works:

1. Content Personalization:

The Explore Page makes use of Instagram's

algorithms to curate content material material based totally on a individual's past interactions, likes, feedback, and the debts they comply with. It objectives to show customers content fabric material they may be in all likelihood to find out attractive.

Chapter 4: Engagement and Community Building

Building a robust and engaged community on Instagram is critical for developing your logo's presence and fostering widespread connections collectively along with your target market. Here are strategies to enhance engagement and community constructing:

1. Respond to Comments and Messages:

Always respond to comments to your

posts and direct messages directly.

Engaging with your aim marketplace demonstrates

which you rate their enter.

2. Encourage User-Generated Content

(UGC):

Encourage your enthusiasts to create and

percentage content cloth fabric related to your brand or

products. Repost UGC with credit score rating to

assist your network.

three. Host Giveaways and Contests:

Organize giveaways and contests that

inspire man or woman participation. Ensure that the

tips are smooth, and prizes are appealing to

your audience.

four. Share Behind-the-Scenes Content:

Give your target market a glimpse within the decrease returned of the

scenes of your corporation or revolutionary approach.

This humanizes your emblem and fosters a

enjoy of connection.

5. Utilize Instagram Stories:

Use Instagram Stories to interact with

your target audience in actual-time. Use features like

polls, questions, and quizzes to interact and

collect comments.

6. Host Q&A Sessions:

Host Q&A training wherein your target audience

can ask questions about your merchandise,

services, or information. This builds be given as real with and

positions you as an expert.

7. Collaborate with Influencers:

Partner with influencers on your area of interest to

reap their engaged fanatics. Influencer collaborations can introduce your brand to a ultra-present day and worried target marketplace.

8. Share User Testimonials and Reviews:

Highlight exceptional character testimonials and

reviews. This no longer best boosts your

credibility however also encourages extra

happy customers to percentage their

testimonies.

9. Consistent Posting Schedule:

Stick to a ordinary posting time desk so

your audience knows even as to expect new

content material. This maintains them engaged and

returning for brought.

10. Use Instagram Live:

Go stay on Instagram to have interaction with

your target marketplace in actual-time. You can solution

questions, communicate current-day topics, or host

interviews.

11. Create Engaging Captions:

Craft compelling and relatable captions that set off your target market to remark and share their mind.

12. Share User Stories:

Share recollections out of your followers or

clients that relate in your brand. This

builds a enjoy of community and inclusivity.

13. Monitor and Analyze Engagement:

Use Instagram Insights to music

engagement metrics. Identify which kinds of

content material material material and posting times generate the maximum

engagement.

14. Organize Virtual Events:

Host webinars, workshops, or live events on Instagram to educate, entertain, or connect to your network.

15. Showcase Customer Success:

Share memories of clients who have achieved fulfillment at the side of your products or services. This demonstrates the charge of your offerings.

Remember that proper engagement and community building take time. Consistency, authenticity, and a honest interest to your goal market's needs and comments are key to nurturing a thriving Instagram network.

5.1 Responding to Comments and Messages on Instagram

Engaging together with your target marketplace thru remarks and direct messages is a important factor of building a strong and lively Instagram network. Here's a way to efficaciously respond to feedback and messages:

Responding to Comments: 1. Reply Promptly: Aim to answer to feedback to your posts as fast as viable, ideally within some hours or an afternoon at maximum. Timely responses show that you value your lovers.

2. Be Grateful: Always unique gratitude for awesome feedback and compliments. A easy "Thank you" can bypass a long way in building goodwill.

3. Acknowledge Questions: If a commentary consists of a query or inquiry, answer it thoroughly and professionally. Provide beneficial records or direct them to the best resource.

four. Use Their Name: If the commenter's call is seen of their profile, customise your reaction by means of manner of way of addressing them with the resource of call. 5. Encourage Engagement: Encourage further engagement with the resource of asking open-ended questions on your replies. This can result in extra comments and discussions.

6. Handle Negative Comments Gracefully: If you get hold of horrific comments or complaint, respond professionally and empathetically. Address concerns and offer solutions privately if important.

7. Limit Emojis and Slang: While emojis and slang can add a non-public contact, keep in mind of your logo's tone and professionalism.

Responding to Direct Messages:

1. Check Your Inbox Regularly: Make it a addiction to check your direct message (DM) inbox each day. Respond to messages right away, mainly the ones from customers or functionality customers.

2. Set Expectations: Consider setting response time expectations on your Instagram bio or automatic welcome message to control user expectations. 3. Personalize Your Greetings: When responding to DMs, use the individual's

call if to be had. Personalized greetings enjoy extra true.

four. Keep Conversations Private: For sensitive or non-public discussions, inspire customers to exchange to e-mail or every other regular platform.

5. Use Quick Replies: Instagram's Quick Replies feature allows you to create pre-written responses for frequently asked questions or not unusual inquiries. This can save time and offer everyday answers. 6. Be Professional: Maintain a expert and respectful tone in all DM interactions, despite the fact that the person is informal or informal. 7. Provide Value: Use direct messages as an possibility to offer rate, whether or not or not it's far answering questions, sharing one-of-a-kind content material material material, or supplying custom designed suggestions.

8. Use Canned Responses Sparingly:While automation can be useful, avoid the usage of canned responses excessively. Overuse have to make interactions experience robotic.

nine. Flag Important Messages: Instagram allows you to mark messages as critical or unread to make certain you do not pass over important inquiries or take a look at-ups.

10. Archive Old Conversations: To hold your inbox prepared, undergo in thoughts archiving antique conversations which might be no longer lively but can also however encompass precious facts.

Remember that responsive and customized engagement fosters a exquisite courting together collectively with your goal marketplace and strengthens your Instagram community. It's a valuable opportunity to show off your brand's self-control to customer service and delight.

five.2 Collaborations and Partnerships on Instagram

Collaborations and partnerships on Instagram can be powerful strategies for growing your emblem, growing visibility, and reaching a much broader audience. Here's the way to approach collaborations efficaciously:

1. Identify Compatible Partners:

Look for human beings or manufacturers whose

values, target marketplace, and content material align

with yours. Compatibility is vital for a

a achievement collaboration.

2. Reach Out with a Clear Proposal:

When drawing close to capability

collaborators, be clear about your dreams,

what you may offer, and what you count on in

go back. A well-described idea makes it

less difficult for others to bear in mind running with

you.

three. Create Mutually Beneficial Content:

Collaborations have to advantage every

events. Plan content this is engaging and

precious in your blended audiences.

Brainstorm mind that exhibit each producers

authentically.

four. Leverage Influencer Marketing:

Partnering with influencers for your area of hobby can introduce your brand to a contemporary and engaged goal marketplace. Ensure that the influencer's values and aim marketplace healthy your emblem.

5. Co-Host Giveaways and Contests:

Running joint giveaways or contests with

collaborators can generate pleasure and

engagement. Require people to comply with

both debts and interact with content material.

6. Cross-Promote:

Promote every different's content cloth and profiles

in posts, reminiscences, or captions. This mutual

merchandising can purpose follower crossovers.

7. Share User-Generated Content:

Encourage your collaborative partners to

percent person-generated content material providing your

emblem. This expands your gain and builds

take transport of as true with via social proof.

eight. Collaborative Takeovers:

Consider taking over each considered one of a kind's

Instagram debts for a day or a particular

occasion. This offers your goal marketplace clean

content material material and insights.

9. Product Collaborations:

Create precise products or services

together and sell them on every

money owed. This can be particularly effective for

corporations in associated niches.

10. Host Instagram Live Sessions:

Go stay together to speak approximately topics of

mutual interest, conduct interviews, or

really engage together with your audiences in

actual-time.

11. Measure and Evaluate:

After a collaboration, study the

consequences. Measure engagement, follower

growth, and different key ordinary usual performance signs and symptoms to evaluate the effect of the partnership.

12. Legal Agreements:

If a collaboration includes massive assets or belongings, don't forget drafting a jail settlement outlining obligations, expectancies, and terms of the partnership. Thirteen. Stay Authentic:

Maintain authenticity in collaborations. Ensure that the content material fabric cloth aligns together with your brand's values and messaging to avoid perplexing or alienating your target market. 14. Long-Term Relationships:

Consider constructing prolonged-term relationships with collaborators who percentage your imaginative and prescient. Repeat collaborations with the same companions can yield stronger effects over time.

15. Be Open to New Ideas:

Stay open to easy collaboration mind and partnerships which could upward push up. The Instagram panorama is constantly evolving, imparting new possibilities.

Collaborations and partnerships can breathe new life into your Instagram advertising and marketing efforts. By running with like-minded human beings and types, you could tap into new audiences, foster engagement, and create content material fabric material that resonates with a broader type of fans.

five.Three Running Contests and Giveaways on Instagram

Contests and giveaways are fairly effective techniques for boosting engagement, growing your follower matter, and generating delight round your brand on Instagram. Here's a step-by manner of-step guide to on foot a fulfillment contests and giveaways:

1. Define Your Goals:

Determine the targets of your contest

or giveaway. Are you aiming to benefit new

fans, sell a ultra-modern product, or surely

improve engagement?

2. Choose the Type of Contest or

Giveaway:

There are severa types of contests and

giveaways, consisting of:

Like and Comment: Participants like

your post and observation to enter.

Tag a Friend: Participants tag buddies

inside the comments.

User-Generated Content (UGC):

Participants create and percent content
material fabric associated

on your logo or merchandise.

Trivia or Quiz: Participants answer questions related to your brand or business enterprise.

Random Draw: Winners are decided on randomly from all entrants.

3. Set Clear Rules and Guidelines:

Create unique recommendations and tips for

your contest or giveaway. Specify get right of entry to

necessities, closing dates, eligibility criteria,

and the range of winners.

four. Choose Prizes: Offer attractive prizes that are applicable to your audience and emblem. Prizes can include products, splendid get admission to, reductions, or even research.

Chapter 5: Using Instagram Analytics for Success

Instagram Analytics presents precious insights into the overall overall performance of your posts, Stories, and normal account. Leveraging those analytics permit you to refine your technique and attain higher consequences on the platform. Here's a manner to make the most of Instagram Analytics:

1. Accessing Instagram Analytics:

To get right of access to Instagram Analytics, you want a enterprise or creator account. Once you've got one, navigate to your profile, faucet the three horizontal lines within the top proper nook, and select "Insights."

2. Overview of Metrics:

Instagram Analytics gives a number of metrics, together with:

Follower Growth: Track the variety of new enthusiasts obtained over the years.

Reach and Impressions: Understand how many customers have visible your content cloth.

Engagement: Measure likes, feedback, stocks, and saves for character posts.

Audience Demographics: Gain insights into your lovers' age, gender, region, and extra.

Content Interactions: See which posts and Stories resonate most along side your goal market.

three. Post Performance Analysis:

Examine the overall overall performance of individual posts and Stories to select out what content material works first rate. Look for styles inside the form of content material material, captions, and posting times that achieve the maximum engagement.

four. Audience Insights:

Use target market demographics to refine your content material material technique. Tailor your posts to cater to the interests and alternatives of your number one goal marketplace.

5. Track Follower Growth:

Keep an eye constant for your follower boom traits. Analyze what strategies coincide with spikes in growth, and find out intervals of decline to cope with capacity issues. 6. Assess Reach and Impressions:

Understand how a protracted manner your content material is undertaking and the way often it's far being viewed. High obtain with low engagement may advocate the need for more compelling content material material material.

7. Engagement Rate:

Calculate your engagement charge by using the usage of dividing modern engagement (likes, remarks, shares) via the amount of lovers. This metric permits gauge content material cloth best and audience interaction.

eight. Content Mix:

Analyze the styles of content material cloth
cloth (photos,

movies, carousels, Stories) that carry out
brilliant.

Adjust your content combination due to this.

nine. Optimize Posting Times:

Use statistics on while your intention market
is maximum

active to time desk posts for max reach

and engagement.

10. Instagram Stories Insights:

Monitor the general overall performance of
your

Stories. Identify which Stories generate the

most views, replies, and engagement.

eleven. Competitor Analysis:

Benchmark your regular normal performance
in opposition to competition or similar money

owed. Identify opportunities to distinguish your content material cloth material. 12. Set Goals and KPIs:

Define clean desires and key performance signs (KPIs) primarily based to your analytics. This will assist you music progress and measure the achievement of your Instagram approach.

13. Experiment and Iterate:

Use insights to test with one in every of a type

content material techniques. Continuously iterate and

refine your method based mostly on what works

exceptional in your intention market.

14. Regular Reporting:

Create regular reviews to track your

improvement and percentage insights collectively with your team or stakeholders. Consistent reporting can

help refine your approach over time.

15. Stay Updated:

Instagram updates its analytics talents

often. Stay informed approximately new metrics

and gadget that may enhance your

information of your target marketplace and

regular overall performance.

By leveraging Instagram Analytics, you

should make records-driven decisions to optimize

your content material, engagement, and regular

Instagram technique, ultimately major to

better consequences and a extra effective presence

at the platform.

6.1 Understanding Instagram Insights

Instagram Insights is a powerful device that gives treasured statistics and analytics approximately your account's performance. Here's a breakdown of key factors of Instagram Insights that will help you recognize and leverage this tool efficiently:

1. Accessing Instagram Insights:

Instagram Insights is to be had to customers with commercial company or author debts. To get right of entry to it, visit your profile, faucet the 3 horizontal strains in the pinnacle proper nook, and select out "Insights."

2. Overview Metrics:

Instagram Insights gives more than a few

metrics, which encompass:

Interactions: Total actions taken on your

account, which include profile visits, net website

clicks, and electronic mail clicks.

Discovery: Reach (the kind of

precise money owed that noticed your content material) and impressions (the overall quantity of times your

content material became displayed).

Content Interactions: Likes, remarks,

shares, and saves in your posts.

Audience Demographics: Insights into

your enthusiasts' age, gender, region, and

at the identical time as they'll be maximum lively.

3. Follower Insights:

The "Followers" tab offers a deeper

knowledge of your target marketplace, along with

at the same time as they're maximum active in the course of the week and day. You can also see your followers'

age variety, gender distribution, and vicinity.

4. Content Insights:

This segment breaks down your posts and

Stories with the aid of the usage of using performance. You can view

metrics for character posts, including reap,

engagement, and saves.

5. Activity Insights:

In the "Activity" phase, you may see how frequently users visited your profile, observed you, and interacted at the aspect of your content material during the last week.

6. Instagram Stories Insights:

Instagram Insights also gives

Story-specific statistics, collectively with attain, exits,

and engagement for every Story. You can see

what number of people considered every a part of your

Story.

7. Promotions Insights:

If you run paid promotions, Instagram

Insights offers statistics on how nicely your classified ads

are appearing, consisting of obtain,

impressions, and moves taken.

8. Exporting Insights:

You can export Insights statistics for in addition

assessment and reporting. This is useful for sharing general normal overall performance metrics with group contributors or stakeholders.

9. Comparisons and Trends:

Instagram Insights allows you to have a observe your modern-day universal performance with beyond data, allowing you to identify inclinations and word how your approach has advanced over time. 10. Audience Growth:

Track the increase of your follower rely and understand how various factors, along with particular posts or promotions, contributed to that growth.

eleven. Audience Behavior:

Insights can show the forms of content material that resonate most along with your target market, helping you refine your content material fabric technique. 12. Instagram Shopping Insights:

If you have got were given had been given a commercial business agency selling merchandise, Instagram Insights can offer information on how often human beings interacted collectively along with your looking for posts and tapped to view product records. Thirteen. Content Insights via Type:

Instagram Insights breaks down your content fabric overall performance through type, which encompass pics, movies, carousel posts, and Stories. 14. Exporting Insights Data:

You can export your Insights facts for extra in-intensity analysis the use of out of doors equipment or software program software.

15. Using Insights for Strategy:

Insights should tell your content material fabric technique. Identify what styles of content material cloth resonate maximum together along with your target marketplace and on the same time as they're most energetic to optimize your posting schedule.

By regularly reviewing and studying Instagram Insights, you can refine your Instagram marketing and advertising and marketing and marketing method, tailor your content cloth in your goal marketplace's alternatives, and make information-pushed selections to gain better results at the platform.

6.2 Understanding key metrics is essential for assessing the overall overall performance of your Instagram account and guiding your social media approach. Here are the essential aspect metrics to expose:

1. Engagement Rate:

Definition: Engagement fee measures

the extent of interaction and interest on your

Instagram content. It typically consists of

likes, remarks, shares, and saves.

Formula: (Total Engagements / Total

Followers) x a hundred

Significance: A immoderate engagement charge

shows that your content material is resonating with

your goal market. It's a sign of active and

concerned enthusiasts.

2. Follower Growth:

Definition: Follower increase tracks how

your follower depend is converting over the years. It

shows the success of your content cloth and

outreach efforts.

Formula: (New Followers Lost

Followers) / Total Followers x 100

Significance: Steady and natural

follower growth is a remarkable sign. Rapid

increase could mean a fulfillment campaigns

or promotions.

3. Reach:

Definition: Reach measures the amount

of particular money owed which have visible your

content material. It allows you apprehend how massive

your content material's distribution is.

Significance: A better gain suggests

that your content cloth fabric is conducting a broader

goal marketplace. It's a precious metric for assessing

content visibility.

4. Impressions:

Definition: Impressions diploma the overall

amount of instances your content cloth fabric has been

taken into consideration, collectively with a couple of views by way of the usage of the

same individual. It displays how often your

content material material is seen.

Significance: A high extensive type of

impressions indicates that your content material cloth is being considered more than one instances. It's important for gauging content fabric reputation.

5. Likes (Hearts):

Definition: Likes represent the amount of

clients who've desired your content material material by using

double-tapping it.

Significance: Likes are a vital

engagement metric. They display that customers

find out your content material material appealing or exciting.

Chapter 6: Paid Advertising On Instagram

Paid advertising on Instagram may be a considerably powerful manner to gain a larger and additional focused target market. Instagram gives numerous advert codecs and targeted on alternatives to help groups sell their services or products. Here's a step-through the use of-step manual to getting started with paid advertising and marketing on Instagram:

1. Create a Business Account:

Ensure you have got were given a business enterprise or creator

account on Instagram. If you don't have one,

you may without issues switch from a non-public

account or create a modern industrial commercial enterprise corporation account.

2. Link to Facebook:

Connect your Instagram account to a Facebook Page. Instagram marketing and marketing and marketing is controlled via Facebook Ads Manager, so this linkage is important.

three. Define Your Advertising Objectives:

Determine your advertising desires.

Instagram offers numerous targets,

which consist of emblem interest, reach,

engagement, web page visitors, app installs, video

perspectives, lead era, and extra. Choose

the one that aligns together together along with your marketing campaign

dreams.

four. Set Your Target Audience:

Use Facebook Ads Manager to define

your goal marketplace. You can specify

demographics, pastimes, behaviors, vicinity,

and extra to obtain the proper humans.

5. Choose Ad Placement:

Decide in which you need your classified ads to seem. Instagram offers diverse ad placements, which include Instagram Feed, Instagram Stories, and the Explore segment. 6. Select Ad Format:

Instagram gives severa advert formats, which include photograph advertisements, video classified ads, carousel ads (more than one pix or films in a unmarried ad), and slideshow commercials (a looping video series). Choose the format that suits your content. 7. Create Compelling Ad Content:

Design is visually attractive and tasty and progressive. Ensure it aligns together along with your advertising and marketing marketing campaign targets and is optimized for cell viewing.

8. Craft a Captivating Caption:

Write a compelling caption that

enhances your ad progressive and

encourages clients to accomplish that. Include a clean call to motion (CTA) that tells customers what you want them to do.

9. Set a Budget and Schedule:

Determine your day by day or lifetime charge range and pick the period of your ad marketing marketing campaign. Facebook Ads Manager offers real-time price range and scheduling alternatives. 10. Optimize for Delivery:

Select optimization options primarily based completely on your campaign aim. For instance, if your reason is conversions, optimize for net net web page conversions.

11. Review and Launch:

Double-test your advert settings, targeted on, and creativity. Once you are glad, click on on at the "Publish" or "Submit" button to release your advert advertising advertising campaign.

12. Monitor and Analyze:

Regularly test the overall universal performance of your advertisements using Facebook Ads Manager. Track metrics together with accumulate, impressions, engagement, click-thru fee (CTR), and conversion rate.

13. A/B Testing:

Experiment with particular ad creatives,

captions, and target market segments to pick out out

what works extraordinary. A/B attempting out allow you to

optimize your advert campaigns.

14. Adjust and Optimize:

Based at the overall overall performance records, make

essential modifications on your ad campaigns.

You can refine your aim market centered on,

tweak and be innovative, and reallocate your

price range.

15. Retargeting:

Implement retargeting campaigns to

benefit clients who've formerly interacted at the side of your emblem on Instagram or your internet net page.

16. Ad Compliance:

Ensure your advertisements have a take a look at Instagram's advertising and marketing and marketing and advertising tips and hints to prevent disapproval or account

guidelines.

Paid advertising on Instagram can be a

effective tool for growing your emblem,

developing internet site site visitors, and riding

conversions. By cautiously planning your

campaigns, concentrated on the right target market, and

reading average performance, you may maximize

the effectiveness of your Instagram classified ads.

7.1 Instagram Ads vs. Organic Posts: Understanding the Di erences

Instagram gives number one techniques for corporations to achieve their intention market: through herbal posts and paid advertising and marketing. Each method has its blessings and serves splendid competencies. Here's a evaluation of Instagram commercials and natural posts:

1. Reach and Visibility:

Instagram Ads:

With Instagram commercials, you may achieve a larger and extra focused target marketplace compared to herbal posts. You can use advanced centered on alternatives to make sure your content is examined to the proper people.

Organic Posts:

Organic obtain is limited to your contemporary fanatics and clients who discover your content cloth fabric via hashtags or discover functions. It can be tough to gain new audiences without paid promoting.

2. Content Control:

Instagram Ads:

You have entire manipulate over the content material, which incorporates the ad format, innovative, caption, and speak to to movement. This permits for quite tailor-made and strategic messaging.

Organic Posts:

While you can manage the content material of herbal posts, they'll now not usually align together collectively together with your advertising and marketing and advertising and marketing and marketing and marketing dreams or reap the right target audience.

three. Targeting Options:

Instagram Ads:

Paid marketing offers sturdy targeting options based totally on demographics, pastimes, behaviors, and extra. You can exactly outline your first-rate target audience.

Organic Posts:

Organic posts rely on your gift fanatics and won't be as specific in phrases of focused on.

four. Ad Formats:

Instagram Ads:

You can select out from numerous ad formats, which incorporates picture advertisements, video commercials, carousel commercials, and Stories commercials. Each format serves a unique motive and presents precise progressive opportunities.

Organic Posts:

Organic posts are confined to the same vintage Instagram publish layout. While you may placed up pics, motion photographs, and carousels, you've got were given fewer alternatives for interactive elements. Five. Call to Action (CTA):

Instagram Ads:

Instagram advertisements will let you encompass clean and actionable CTAs like "Shop Now," "Learn More," "Sign Up," or "Book Now," directing clients to take specific actions.

Organic Posts:

Organic posts can encompass CTAs in captions, however they will no longer be as visually prominent or compelling as the ones in commercials. 6. Analytics and Insights:

Instagram Ads:

Paid marketing presents particular analytics and insights thru Instagram Insights and Facebook Ads Manager. You can tune metrics collectively with achieve, engagement, click on on on-through price, and conversion rate.

Organic Posts:

Organic posts offer restrained insights, commonly targeted on likes, remarks, and saves. You have lots less records to investigate and optimize your approach.

7. Cost:

Instagram Ads:

Paid advertising on Instagram requires a fee variety. The charge is predicated upon on various factors, which includes your targeted on, bid method, and competition.

Organic Posts:

Organic posts are free. However, they may require extra time and effort to attain large acquire and engagement.

eight. Speed and Timing:

Instagram Ads:

Ads can be launched quick and scheduled to run at precise instances, making them best for time-touchy promotions or sports.

Organic Posts:

Organic posts are problem to the chronological set of policies, and their visibility also can rely on whilst you post.

In summary, Instagram classified ads are a powerful device for undertaking a selected audience, driving conversions, and accomplishing specific advertising goals. Organic posts are treasured for constructing and attractive at the side of your modern-day-day goal marketplace however may moreover have obstacles in phrases of achieve and manage. Many businesses discover achievement via combining each techniques of their Instagram advertising approach, the usage of natural posts for network-constructing and paid advertising and marketing and advertising for centered campaigns.

7.2 Creating Instagram Ads (Promotions)

Creating Instagram commercials, additionally known as promotions, consists of using

Facebook Ads Manager to layout, goal, and launch your advert campaigns on the Instagram platform. Here's a step-with the useful resource of way of-step manual at the manner to create Instagram advertisements:

1. Access Facebook Ads Manager:

Log in on your Facebook Ads Manager

2. Choose Your Campaign Objective:

Click the "Create" button to start a cutting-edge-day

campaign. Select your advertising marketing campaign intention.

Instagram gives severa goals, which incorporates

emblem attention, gather, engagement, internet site traffic,

app installs, and greater. Choose the simplest that

aligns together along with your goals.

3. Define Your Target Audience:

In the advert set advent section, you can outline

your aim marketplace. Specify demographics,

area, hobbies, behaviors, and different

standards to obtain the right human beings.

four. Select Ad Placements:

Choose wherein you need your Instagram

commercials to seem. You can pick out "Automatic

Placements," which we must Facebook optimize

placement based totally totally on performance, or

manually pick "Edit Placements" to pick

Instagram specifically.

five. Set Your Budget and Schedule:

Determine your each day or lifetime fee range

for the advertising and marketing marketing campaign. You can set a price variety cap

and agenda your commercials to run at some point of specific

days and times.

6. Choose Your Ad Format:

Instagram offers numerous ad formats, which incorporates:

Photo Ads: Single pix with captions.

Video Ads: Short motion images with captions.

Carousel Ads: Multiple pix or films in a single ad, allowing customers to swipe via.

Stories Ads: Full-display vertical advertisements that appear among users' Stories.

Slideshow Ads: Lightweight video commercials constructed from a chain of photographs.

7. Create Ad Creative:

Design your ad innovative in keeping with your selected layout. Upload photographs or films, write compelling advert copy, and include a clean name to motion (CTA). Ensure that your modern aligns along side your campaign purpose and goal market.

8. Add a Destination Link:

Include a link to the landing net web page or

vacation spot you need customers to go to whilst

they click on on for your ad. Make quality the hyperlink is

relevant for your advertising and marketing marketing marketing campaign cause.

nine. Review and Confirm:

Review all the information of your ad

marketing campaign, on the aspect of centered on, price range, advert

layout, and creative. Ensure everything is

installation efficiently.

10. Track and Measure:

Once your Instagram classified ads are live, use

Facebook Ads Manager to reveal their

overall performance. Track metrics which incorporates reach,

impressions, engagement, click-through fee

(CTR), and conversion rate.

11. Optimize Your Campaign:

Regularly analyze your ad advertising and marketing marketing campaign's

common overall performance information. Make adjustments based totally mostly on what's operating and what is now not. Experiment with precise advert innovative, focused on alternatives, and ad codecs to optimize your campaigns over the years.

12. Ad Compliance:

Ensure that your classified ads check Instagram's advertising guidelines and hints to save you disapproval or account regulations.

thirteen. Experiment with A/B Testing:

To high-quality-music your campaigns, hold in thoughts

strolling A/B tests with unique ad

versions to look which performs nice. This

permit you to refine your advert innovative,

focused on, and messaging.

14. Scale Successful Campaigns:

If you find that nice campaigns are

handing over strong effects, bear in mind scaling them with the aid of developing your rate variety or expanding your concentrated on.

By following those steps, you may create

effective Instagram commercials that attain your

favored target marketplace and help you obtain your

advertising objectives on the platform.

Regularly show and optimize your

campaigns to maximise their impact.

7.Three Targeting Your Audience in Instagram Ads

Targeting the right target market is important for the achievement of your Instagram advert campaigns. Instagram gives robust centered on alternatives through Facebook Ads Manager. Here's the manner to correctly target your target market:

1. Location:

Define the geographical place in which you need your commercials to be shown. You can goal a selected u . S ., town, region, or maybe a radius spherical a selected area. 2. Demographics:

Specify demographic criteria which encompass age, gender, language, and training level. This allows you reach clients who in shape your tremendous patron profile.

three. Interests and Behaviors:

Narrow down your goal marketplace based totally on

their pursuits, interests, and behaviors. You

can goal customers interested in unique subjects,

industries, or sports sports.

four. Detailed Targeting:

Utilize precise focused on alternatives to

refine your target market further. This includes

focused on customers based totally on their connections,

existence occasions, challenge titles, and extra.

five. Custom Audiences:

Create custom audiences through uploading

lists of your modern-day clients' email

addresses or cellphone numbers. This allows

you to goal clients who are already acquainted

collectively with your emblem.

6. Lookalike Audiences:

Build lookalike audiences based completely in your

custom target market lists. Facebook will

discover customers who share comparable

tendencies and pastimes together collectively along with your modern clients.

7. Behavioral Targeting:

Target clients primarily based definitely totally on their on-line

conduct, in conjunction with shopping for conduct, device

utilization, adventure alternatives, and further.

eight. Connection Type:

Specify whether or no longer you need to goal customers

associated with your Instagram account, customers who have engaged with your app or sports activities, or exclude particular instructions.

Chapter 7: Instagram Shopping

Instagram Shopping is a effective characteristic that lets in organizations to showcase their products and permit direct purchasing for on the platform. Here's a entire guide at the way to use Instagram Shopping efficiently:

1. Set Up Your Instagram Business Account:

Ensure that you have a corporation or creator account on Instagram. You can convert your present account or create a modern-day one.

2. Meet Eligibility Requirements:

To use Instagram Shopping, your

business business enterprise should meet certain requirements, consisting of going for walks in a supported market, adhering to Instagram's exchange tips, and having an eligible product category. Three. Connect to a Facebook Catalog:

To feature merchandise on Instagram, you want to create and manage a product catalog on Facebook. Use Facebook Commerce Manager to installation your catalog and hyperlink it on your Instagram account.

4. Add Product Tags:

Once your catalog is set up, you may begin tagging your products in posts and Stories. To do this, create a ultra-modern post or Story and select the product you need to tag. Users can faucet at the tags to view product statistics. Five. Utilize Instagram Shop:

Instagram Shop is a committed buying excursion spot in the Instagram app. Ensure that your product catalog is blanketed with Instagram Shop so clients can without issue discover and find out your products.

6. Enable Instagram Checkout:

Instagram Checkout lets in clients to finish their purchases with out leaving the app. To permit this feature, art work with Instagram's partners or use Instagram's neighborhood checkout device if to be had for your market.

7. Craft Engaging Product Descriptions:

When tagging products, embody informative and appealing descriptions that encourage clients to find out and buy. Highlight key capabilities and advantages.

8. Use High-Quality Imagery:

Visual content material is vital. Use immoderate-selection photos and films that showcase your merchandise from amazing angles and in numerous settings.

nine. Leverage Stories and IGTV:

Don't restrict your self to normal posts. Use

Instagram Stories and IGTV to feature

products and provide a more immersive

purchasing revel in.

10. Implement Shopping Ads:

Instagram offers Shopping Ads that

allow you to promote your products to a

wider target marketplace. These advertisements can seem in

customers' feeds or Stories.

11. Engage with Users:

Encourage individual-generated content material material by means of manner of the use of

sharing client opinions and snap shots.

Engage with comments and messages

right away to offer resource and construct bear in mind.

12. Use Hashtags and Explore:

Include relevant hashtags and geotags to

increase the discoverability of your products. Utilize Instagram's Explore feature to attain new potential clients.

thirteen. Analyze Performance:

Regularly evaluation Instagram Insights to show the general overall performance of your buying posts and Stories. Track metrics like clicks, impressions, and conversion fee.

14. Run Promotions and Campaigns:

Create unique promotions or campaigns to force website site visitors for your Instagram Shop and growth sales in a few unspecified time inside the future of peak seasons or occasions. 15. Stay Compliant:

Adhere to Instagram's trade guidelines and tips to ensure your purchasing experience complies with their policies.

sixteen. Explore New Features:

Stay up to date with Instagram's evolving shopping for abilities and tools. Instagram is continually along with new capabilities to

enhance the shopping for enjoy.

Instagram Shopping gives organizations a

precise possibility to hook up with

customers and force profits immediately at the

platform. By following the ones steps and

staying engaged together together with your target market, you

can correctly leverage Instagram as a

buying holiday spot on your emblem.

eight.1 Setting Up Instagram Shopping: A Step-via-Step Guide

Instagram Shopping permits groups to characteristic and promote products right now on their Instagram profiles. Setting it up requires a few steps to make certain your account and products are eligible. Here's a complete manual:

1. Eligibility Check:Before you begin, ensure your

industrial business enterprise meets Instagram's eligibility

necessities:

Operate in a supported marketplace.

Comply with Instagram's trade

policies.

Have an eligible product elegance.

2. Convert to a Business or Creator Account:

If you haven't already, transfer your Instagram account to a commercial enterprise or creator account. Go for your account settings and select out "Switch to Professional Account." three. Connect to a Facebook Page:

Your Instagram corporation account need to be related to a Facebook Page. If you don't have a Facebook Page for your business organisation, create one.

4. Verify Your Business:

To enhance your credibility, don't forget

verifying your Instagram industrial employer account.

This is non-obligatory but can collect believe with

capacity customers.

5. Create a Facebook Catalog:

Instagram Shopping is based on a Facebook catalog to show off your products. Use Facebook Commerce Manager to set up your catalog:

Go to Facebook Commerce Manager (business enterprise.Facebook.Com/commerce_manager/).

Create a brand new catalog and choose the "E-commerce" opportunity.

Add your products and product information to the catalog. Ensure that product information is correct, along side pricing and availability.

6. Add Shopping Tags:

Once your catalog is installation, you may begin tagging merchandise on your Instagram posts and Stories. Here's how:

Create a modern day placed up or Story as traditional.

When you upload an picture, you may see an choice to "Tag Products."

Tap on the picture to select out out the goods you want to tag.

Enter product names or pick out from your catalog.

Click "Done" and percent your located up or Story.

7. Submit for Review:

After tagging merchandise in posts, your

account can be reviewed thru Instagram to make certain compliance with their policies. This evaluation can take a few days to complete. Eight. Enable Instagram Shopping:

Once your account is permitted, you may get keep of a notification to allow Instagram Shopping. Go on your settings, and beneath "Business," pick "Shopping."

nine. Create a Shop Tab:

A "Shop" tab may be mechanically delivered in your Instagram profile. This is in which users can view all of your tagged products. 10. Enable Instagram Checkout

(Optional):

If Instagram Checkout is to be had in

your market, you can allow it to allow clients

to shop for products directly at the

platform.

eleven. Craft Engaging Product Descriptions:

When tagging products, offer compelling and informative descriptions to encourage clients to find out and purchase.

12. Regularly Update Your Catalog:

Keep your catalog updated with the

ultra-present day merchandise, pricing, and availability.

13. Analyze Performance:

Use Instagram Insights to song the

trendy performance of your Shopping posts.

Monitor metrics like clicks, impressions,

and conversion rate.

14. Engage with Users:

Respond to comments and messages

at once to provide manual and collect remember

with your audience.

15. Promote Your Instagram Shop:

Share your Instagram Shop to your

distinct social media channels and web sites to

growth visibility.

By following those steps and retaining a properly-organized product catalog, you could correctly set up Instagram Shopping and make it much less difficult for customers to find out and preserve for your merchandise at once out of your Instagram profile.

8.2 Tagging Products in Instagram Posts and Stories: A Step-thru-Step Guide

Tagging products to your Instagram posts and Stories is a powerful way to reveal off and promote your products for your target marketplace. Here's a step-by means of the use of the usage of-step guide on a manner to do it:

Tagging Products in Instagram Posts: 1. Create a New Post:

Open the Instagram app and tap the '+' button to create a brand new located up.

2. Choose or Upload a Photo:

Select a image out of your gallery or take a cutting-edge-day one. Ensure that this image functions the product you want to tag.

three. Add a Caption and Filters:

Write a captivating caption in your put up.

Make it descriptive and include relevant

hashtags if favored. You also can practice

filters and edit the picture as you normally

could.

four. Tag Products:

Tap at the image to feature product tags.

You'll see an preference that looks like a small

searching for bag icon. Tap on it.

five. Select the Product:

A listing of products from your connected Facebook catalog will appear. Choose the product you want to tag within the picture. 6. Position the Tag:

Drag the product tag to the proper region on the photograph. Ensure it's miles positioned wherein customers can without problem see and tap on it. 7. Add More Products (Optional):

If you have got were given multiple products within the identical photo, repeat the tagging way for each product.

8. Complete Your Post:

Finish crafting your submit through including any

more content material, which includes mentions,

hashtags, or area tags.

9. Share Your Post:

Once you're satisfied together with your located up, tap

"Share" to place up it. Users can now tap at the product tags to view data and make purchases.

Tagging Products in Instagram Stories:

1. Create a New Story:

Open the Instagram app and swipe right

on your own home show or tap your profile

picture to create a contemporary Story.

2. Capture or Select Content:

Capture a photo or video for your Story

or choose one from your gallery.

3. Add Product Sticker:

In the Story enhancing interface, tap the

decal icon (seems like a square smiley face)

on the pinnacle.

4. Select the Product Sticker:

In the sticky label alternatives, locate and faucet the

"Product" sticker.

5. Choose the Product:

Select the product out of your catalog that

you want to characteristic to your Story.

6. Position the Sticker:

Place the product decal in a superb

place inside your Story. Users can tap on

it to view records.

7. Customize and Share:

Customize your Story as preferred with

textual content, drawings, or exclusive stickers. Once your

Story is ready, percent it alongside facet your fanatics.

8. Viewing and Shopping:

When site visitors tap at the product sticker

to your Story, they'll see product records,

collectively with the decision and rate. They can tap

all over again to go to your Instagram Shop and make

a purchase.

By following the ones steps, you may

effectively tag merchandise in each your Instagram posts and Stories, making it available to your purpose market to find out and shop to your products directly from your content fabric cloth. This feature can significantly raise your e-exchange efforts on the platform.

eight.Three Creating Shoppable Posts on Instagram: A Step-via-Step Guide

Shoppable posts on Instagram permit businesses to tag products in their pictures and permit clients to hold right now from their posts. Here's a comprehensive manual on a way to create shoppable posts:

1. Eligibility Check:

Ensure that your business organisation meets

Instagram's eligibility requirements for buying capabilities. You must perform in a supported market, comply with trade policies, and function merchandise in an eligible magnificence. 2. Convert to a Business Account:

If your Instagram account is not already a business organization or writer account, convert it with the useful resource of going to your account settings and choosing "Switch to Professional Account."

3. Connect to a Facebook Page:

Link your Instagram commercial enterprise commercial enterprise organisation account to a Facebook Page associated with your corporation. If you don't have one, create a Facebook Page.

4. Verify Your Business (Optional):

While optionally available, recall verifying your Instagram business business employer account to decorate credibility.

5. Set Up a Facebook Catalog:

To create shoppable posts, you want a Facebook catalog. Use Facebook Commerce Manager to installation and manage your product catalog.

Go to Facebook Commerce Manager (business employer.Facebook.Com/commerce_manage r /).

Create a today's catalog and choose out the "E-exchange" alternative.

Add your products, which incorporates records like product names, descriptions, costs, and photographs.

6. Ensure Product Availability:

Make nice that your product catalog correctly suggests product availability and pricing.

7. Connect Instagram Shopping:

After installing your catalog, join it to Instagram Shopping.

Go on your Instagram profile settings.

Under "Business," pick out out "Shopping" and comply with the activates to hyperlink your catalog.

Chapter 8: What Motivates You?

Instagram is one of the great social systems to increase your emblem and make profits, even if you're a amateur in on-line advertising. But allow's get a few element right away: it's going to nevertheless be a hustle. It is probably first-rate to put in fantastic try to generate enough momentum in your account. That's why you want to connect with your reason for beginning this route. If you want clarity on why you are doing this and what motivates you, the shortage of engagement and increase certain to stand up in the early degrees of your journey will purpose you to surrender too quickly.

You will often see critiques from small and large producers displaying how fast they grew on a social community or how loopy their return on funding changed into for a selected social media advertising and marketing and advertising marketing campaign. It's smooth to assume the same will rise up to you. I'm sorry to burst your bubble. It may not.

You may not bypass from zero to Instagram famous in a few weeks or months. If it virtually is why you picked up this ebook, you need to locate that shape of "get wealthy short" mentality a few specific area. The reality of doing commercial enterprise organization is that you not often have that stroke of fulfillment and experience organization miracles. The elegant rule of thumb is the gradual grind and assemble-as a lot as what's going to ultimately grow to be a big success. So, buckle up and anchor yourself within the element that motivates you. Some human beings are recommended via their business organisation desires. Others care approximately converting their lifestyles or turning into social media influencers. Whatever your "WHY" might be, hook up with it and maintain your self grounded.

Why Use Instagram?

Another question you can need to reply is why you're choosing to broaden your Instagram channel. Why not YouTube or

LinkedIn? Give yourself a smooth option to this. I can percentage with you why I started out the usage of Instagram to market my business corporation, and I moreover have motives given to me via pals and college college students of my on-line guides.

Instagram is easy and smooth to apply. Compared to different channels, the simplicity and aesthetics of the systems are very attractive to stop-customers. That leads me to my 2nd component. Instagram has intense engagement levels. Compared to special channels alongside aspect Facebook and Twitter, you could be a brand-new account and although get an target marketplace discovering and liking your content material. For a solopreneur or start-up, this type of natural engagement is precious.

Instagram is understood for nurturing and launching influencers correctly. Suppose you dream of becoming a social media influencer. In that case, Instagram is one of the great places to construct your target market. Brands already recognize and price range for influencer advertising and marketing in 2021, and audiences engage more with influencers they recognize, like, and accept as true with. Making a worthwhile profession on Instagram is in particular probable, even in case you're a stay-at-home mom or a suffering artist, and so that you can result in tremendous monetary freedom.

Partnering with influencers is more available on Instagram for business corporation owners. The turn aspect of that influencer advertising and advertising and advertising and marketing idea is that as organization owners and concept leaders, we are able to fast get our account within the front of a modern-day-day and engaged target market without breaking the monetary organization. There are extremely good tiers of influencers, every with its private pricing options. You can also moreover want to spend zero cash, a few hundred greenbacks, or severa thousand, relying on your price range and the relationships you construct. The influencer can sell your emblem, merchandise, or services to boom earnings. More on influencers and influencer advertising later.

You ought to make cash straight away from Instagram. As a business organization owner, income is excellent to me. Instagram might be very attractive due to the reality, through product placements, we can add tags to products in our pictures with hyperlinks that encompass product descriptions, costs, and the capacity to "preserve now." That technique a customer can move from Instagram in your online shop in seconds, major to profits. The remarkable element is over seventy percent of clients file they revel in shopping products via social media. So, what are you seeking out? Start making plans the way to engage human beings and energy web site traffic in your checkout net net web page.

Instagram Goal Setting

Goal placing might be acquainted in case you've invested sufficient time on-line or in private improvement programs. With a goal to motive for, measuring improvement or maybe assignment success is extra reachable. Think of it like this... If you get into your car and start the usage of west, you could pass all of the time because of the reality "west" have to take you anywhere. Eventually, you can run out of fuel, the automobile will smash down, or you can get worn-out and give up with none experience of delight.

To enjoy the success and achievement we crave, purpose putting is important in our personal and professional lives. This is not a session on individual fulfillment and pleasure, however, so if you're however pressured approximately why you want goals, I suggest getting a ebook from a guru like Jack Canfield, Brian Tracy, John Assaraf, or this type of online specialists who teach that stuff. Setting the proper dreams for our Instagram achievement and brand growth will permit us to tune development, display screen improvement, and decide what works and what does now not. It will deliver us a revel in of direction and a focusing aspect, that's critical within the noisy social media worldwide. It may even allow us to challenge ourselves and keep away from falling for the colorful item syndrome that commonly distracts many social media marketers.

If you need to discover ways to set your social media dreams, right here is a few issue simple you can have a look at.

First, I want you to decide and align your social media dreams together together with your industrial organisation desires. For instance, your enterprise goal might be to increase emblem hobby. In that case, a outstanding social media intention can be to increase natural gain. Coschedule created a exquisite guiding precept you could use as a reference. For the sake of convenience, I am sharing their primary outline below.

Increasing online earnings (Business Objective) can align with tracking conversions from social referrals.

Boosting logo loyalty (Business Objective) can align with tracking the range of new subscribers from Instagram. Increasing sales from new merchandise launched (Business Objective) can align with monitoring conversions from Product Campaigns on Instagram. This is, of path, just a guiding principle when you have already were given a agency.

The 2d thing you need to do is about your S.M.A.R.T (Specific Measurable Aspirational Relevant Timely) dreams. How do you try this on Instagram? By surely defining what you want to accumulate inside a specific time frame. For example, in case you're a personal teacher searching out to use Instagram to collect new customers, then a exquisite S.M.A.R.T. Intention may be to convert ten appointments internal 30 days by manner of posting as soon as an afternoon on Instagram feed and 3 instances a day on Stories with a clean name-to-action. My paid ads fee range is $10 constant with day, which runs a advertising and marketing marketing campaign main to my touchdown page with the "e-book free consultation now" button. The more unique your reason, the higher. If you are extra inquisitive about developing fans, then your first goal need to replicate that.

The 1/three hassle to do in advance than you entire setting your desires for Instagram is to make clear what sort of a intention you'll interest on to fulfill that widespread business organization objective. Here's why. Marketing is deep. You can both create a advertising advertising and marketing marketing campaign for branding or promoting, but you may not often hit each nicely. Unfortunately, few human beings apprehend the difference among branding and selling, so most social media content cloth comes at some stage in as spammy.

To help you stand out for all of the proper motives, I encourage you to have a healthful mixture of branding and selling content to your Instagram feed. Your social media approach need to encompass every components due to the truth humans will interact together together together with your account at first-rate factors in their looking for adventure. It might be high-quality to have branding and promoting to thrive, so get modern with this.

Since you're in the early levels of commercial enterprise business enterprise development on Instagram, you must have a number one business enterprise aim with a social media cause that aligns with that purpose. Then, you need to similarly ruin down that social media intention into milestones. So, going decrease lower back to the non-public trainer example. He should smash down the purpose of selling ten appointments further (mainly if he is without a doubt commenced out building up his Instagram account) into smaller milestones. He must damage it all of the way right all the way down to what number of fans he will want and what degree of engagement he may be searching out earlier than shifting that focus on market into asking them to test out his landing web page and e-book a consultation. Then, he may also want to do branding and conversion dreams, excited through that identical regular aim and getting ten new customer appointments.

Remember, branding need to be finished constantly. It need to be focused on giving. Goals for branding encompass increasing follower rely, attain, likes, stocks, comments, mentions, DMs, and saves. Most of this takes place organically and over a protracted duration. It may require each day posts, masses of studies, and identifying what your target market needs and wherein they are so that you can engage with them and pull them into your global. If, as an example, you want to develop your account to 100,000 fans in 3 hundred and sixty five days, that could be a branding purpose. There are movement steps you want to take to make that take vicinity.

On Instagram, we charge plenty the extent of engagement. The greater human beings remark, reply to Stories with a talk, direct message you, and coronary heart your stuff, the more you may recognize you are growing.

Regarding conversions that purpose earnings, the first-rate method is soft selling. Direct (difficult promoting) only works on social media, in particular Instagram. People need to be stored from being sold.

Chapter 9: You Need a Niche

Whenever deciding on an opening comes up, I continuously obtain mixed reactions. Some humans get it right away, whilst others anticipate I am suggesting they restrict their creativity. There became a time whilst social media modified into more youthful and unsaturated with noisemakers. Anyone with a outstanding logo and powerful message need to stand out proper now. Those days are long gone.

Social media is reaching adulthood, and at the same time as networks like Instagram begin to boast the numbers presently suggested (over 1 billion customers), it is time to take a one-of-a-kind approach. The riches are inside the niches. You need to determine out your location of interest to construct some element huge on Instagram or any superb social community.

Why Niching Down Is So Important.

I guess you're asking yourself why it's critical to vicinity of interest down. It's a fantastic question, and you may regularly pay interest various solutions. Some specialists declare niching down is important as it enables make clear your message and brand identification. That's proper. Others will let you know that niching down allows you to fast set up your self as an expert in a specific challenge depend, as a manner to develop your following quicker. That is likewise actual. For me, the whole concept of niching down has grow to be critical because of the shift in purchaser behavior.

In current-day years, we have were given visible a upward push, stabilization, and a drop in social media usage in extra large networks. Please do not misunderstand; I am now not saying there are not any humans on Facebook, Twitter, Instagram, and a number of those massive social networks. Data proves that the numbers are however first rate. But regardless of boasting large numbers, the drop continues, and customers are starting to sluggish down and chorus from attractive an excessive amount of on those huge networks.

Instead, they choose smaller and additional personalized celebration areas where direct touch with like-minded human beings feels much less complex. As a result, advertising and advertising on social media is taking on a state-of-the-art look, and those who are winning are the organisation owners and influencers centered on a particular location of hobby.

When you niche down, you're not permanently cutting your self off from distinct areas of hobby you'll probably have. Instead, you're laser-focused on a unmarried situation count or place of records that acts as a beacon for like-minded those who care about that identical problem. By niching down your odds of fame out, reaching your audience, and generating better engagement significantly boom. Whether you are an entrepreneur or influencer, that on my own can shave down the journey of turning into a hit on Instagram.

Many a fulfillment Instagrammers have shared testimonies of processes they were given began out. Their content material material modified into all over the vicinity. They tried to be triumphant with the useful aid of drawing in a massive audience, but it didn't pan out. But after selecting a spot and drilling all the way down to that trouble rely, matters started out shifting as they noticed their tribe forming. It makes for a very effective advertising and marketing and marketing and advertising and marketing approach.

Some people will at once examine the number one few paragraphs and realise what vicinity of interest to visit if this is you; congratulations! I struggled for numerous months in advance than figuring out what have to emerge as my place of hobby due to the truth I had such loads of passions and special skills. I labored in numerous industries and cherished organisation, personal improvement, DIY, and guitar playing. As you could recall, I needed help to hobby on one location of interest for Instagram. If you're multi-talented and multi-passionate, then do not worry. You're no longer by myself. This chapter will provide a guiding principle that will help you hone in and slender down your popularity.

Instagram Niches

There are masses of niches on Instagram, and I'm certain the numbers will keep developing. That technique some element place of hobby you choose out, there is in all likelihood to be a geared up-built target audience and some competition. Trust me, you need opposition; I will offer an reason behind why later. If you are beginning your Instagram account to generate earnings, you need to ensure the vicinity of interest is worthwhile. But do now not select out a gap simply as it's a cash-maker! Here are some of the famous niches:

Lifestyle

The manner of lifestyles area of interest is prepared showcasing how exquisite and inspiring your existence is. It's approximately sharing your evaluations, mind, and truth. People love being attentive to brilliant memories and envisioning themselves as part of them. If you have were given a few issue that would wow your fans, make human beings desire they were on your shoes, or encourage them to assume outside the sphere, then this place of hobby might be for you.

Food and cooking

Who might now not love tremendous meals? Food will generally be a huge part of our lives no matter how advanced we turn out to be as civilized people. That's why Instagram favors the meals place of interest hundreds. Cooking maintains to gain recognition on the platform as humans percent recipes, cooking pointers, tutorials, and further. If your love is in meals, no matter how unknown your shape of delicacies, you can build a tribe round your topic as extended because it's correct food and exceptional content.

Business

This might be your place of hobby if you love the area of begin-ups, small agencies, and entrepreneurship. Thanks to the Internet, such a number of business enterprise opportunities can purpose earnings. If cash-making is a passion, you may moreover create an account sharing thoughts, guidelines, and motivation so your lovers may want to make coins and gain economic freedom.

Fashion

Fashion niches are booming on Instagram, and with suitable cause. Brands of all sizes make investments a vast sum of money at the platform, and users flock to those stunning money owed to get stimulated, entertained, and even informed on how they need to appearance. People care about their appearance or maybe more, in order that they need to apprehend what celebrities placed on. If you're obsessed with fashion or have revel in in this enterprise, this is probably properly worth it slow as a equipped target market is prepared to look what you could provide.

Beauty

More famous than fashion on Instagram is beauty. Over 96% of all beauty manufacturers have invested in a sturdy Instagram presence. It's in all likelihood due to the reality many teens and women love interacting with splendor products on Instagram. Users want to look tutorials, beauty tips, product opinions, and some component else you can put together dinner dinner up. Creativity and authenticity are going to be crucial proper right here. The more unique your content material cloth, the better it will carry out.

Health and Fitness

Many humans have prioritized health and nicely-being, especially for the reason that 2020 pandemic. So, it ought to now not be sudden that the fitness and fitness region of interest is worthwhile. It can be a subset of fitness or most effective centered on vitamins. You can expand and monetize your facts with creativity and hard artwork, no matter your preference.

Animals

People on Instagram love pets. Some money owed committed to animals (consisting of pets) have end up so popular they outshine human celebrities. So, if you're obsessed on any creature, it's miles in all likelihood that you can develop a decent following and fan base spherical your non-human pal.

Memes

Instagram is entire of memes. They are terrific, short to create, and the appropriate viral content recipe. If you virtually have a talent for making your buddies chortle or want to curate memes all through the internet, this might be a wonderful vicinity of interest on Instagram.

Travel

Travel is large on Instagram. Some of these debts have big followings, and all they do is put up breathtaking snap shots of an area you have in no manner even heard of and in all likelihood can not manage to pay for to excursion to. That's perhaps why people comply with the ones debts. It gives them a sense of adventure, aspiration, and escapism from their little cubicle. These sorts of bills supply the area's outstanding to the journey fanatic. If you like to journey or dream of travelling whole-time, beginning an records of your very own is a exquisite concept. Share your adventure images, studies, and love for our planet with the Instagram community, and they will praise you with masses of engagement.

Motivational costs

Another notable well-known location of hobby that everyone can start is motivational. If you're a fan of amassing inspiring and motivational rates from the greats, then, by way of all method, move for it. Some debts on

Instagram have amassed together crazy followings via posting lovable prices that make people enjoy top notch. It's like a brief coffee shot for personal development addicts.

Crafts and DIY

Have you generally had a knack for solving matters yourself? Do people call you when they want a home made remedy of a few kind? Then, maintain in mind growing an account in which you percent your passion and capabilities. DIY money owed are quite extremely good and garner first-rate followings. Building topics along side your hands and sharing them together collectively with your tribe is not just profitable. It's additionally a terrific way to monetize your account.

If you've got long past through this listing and felt very well out of location because of the reality none of it resonates with what you want to create on Instagram, do no longer melancholy simply however. While I encourage you to select out a gap with a big sufficient intention market, I understand that specific niches have small followings however nevertheless need to artwork. So, if no longer one of the above felt warm sufficient, check out a few examples on Instagram money owed which are doing properly, notwithstanding the fact that they serve a tiny target market.

Famous Instagram Accounts In Various Niches

If you generally geek out on subjects and pastimes that depart your circle of relatives burdened, those debts want to inspire you to move after your type of people and make your Instagram account a success tale.

Vegan and plant-based totally completely meals

Food is a large category on Instagram, however veganism is not. Yet, you could still create a wholesome target market and get Instagram well-known from this area of interest. A wonderful example is Kate Jenkins, who has an account dedicated to vegan recipes which can be easy to make. She receives a wonderful engagement with every placed up.

Another outstanding instance is dietician Catherine, who shares easy vegan recipes, because the control suggests. With 300K enthusiasts and posts getting upwards of four,000 likes each, Catherine is an tremendous example of ways a small area of interest will pay off big time. Https://elisedarma.Com/blog/tiny-niches-instagram

He's a lovely dog-have become-entrepreneur. I did not make up that come to be aware of. I snagged it from Jiffpom, who has emerge as an influencer on Instagram with over 10 million fans. He has even gained awards and receives featured on media shops together with Fox News. If you have a lovely pup that may entertain your audience, why not region of hobby proper down to that?

Disney

I guess you didn't see that one coming! Yes, Disney themed Instagram account is a actual area of interest. It's tiny however will but make you coins and get you fans. For instance, Kait Killebrew has an account centered essentially on Disney. Instead of a normal tour account, she satisfactory talks about the Disney worldwide. She's got over 5K fanatics, and positive, that doesn't make her a mega influencer, but it does supply her enough have an impact on to receives a fee sponsorship gigs.

Brands that promote products related to Disney now need to paintings with Kait due to the reality they apprehend her aim marketplace is right, hyper-engaged, and reliable to that kind of life-style. It might also appear wild to assume one of these tiny place of hobby is nicely really worth pursuing, however the consequences do not lie.

Search Engine Optimization (seo)

All groups need to seem at the number one internet page of Google. If your superpower and functionality display others the manner to try this, why not create an account round seek engine advertising? You likely might not have loopy numbers as that is a smaller niche, however you may nonetheless do superb in phrases of engagement and earnings. For example, @conqueryourcontent focuses on all matters seek engine advertising-related. She has a following of over 2K, which makes her a micro-influencer. According to the quest engine advertising experts, the small following brings her notable leads, and she or he's constantly producing new duties each month from her Instagram advertising and marketing and advertising and marketing.

Whether you have got already got an account, now's the time to assemble that proper basis. Let the examples and training I've shared inspire you to pick out the area of hobby you will efficiently art work on over the upcoming months and years. To help you do it the right way, observe the steps beneath.

How To Choose Your Niche The Right Way

Step #1: Begin at the side of your passions, competencies, and skills.

As I said, you will be doing this for a long term. Before that account can generate have an effect on and sales for you, there may be an entire lot of time, belongings, and electricity investment on your stop, so it makes feel to do what you already experience.

That's why you want to discover your strengths, passions, and pastimes. Make this approach impactful by means of the use of going via the following questions with me. You can write the answers on a Google record or a notepad—listing as many as you may think approximately.

What challenge consider do you maximum revel in speaking about with pals and own family? You have to flow into on for hours in the occasion that they had let you.

How do you need to spend your unfastened time?

What pursuits have you ever ever had due to the reality youth?

What did you want to do at the equal time as you've got been nine? How about selling lemonade or developing comedian characters?

What topics do you revel in studying? Look on the blogs, magazines, and social media bills you take a look at.

What talents have you ever knowledgeable on which you're appropriate at?

Is there a few issue human beings like to get your recommendation on? It might be make-up tips, film recommendations, or a few aspect else.

Step #2: Do aggressive research.

Once you pick out what you are interested in posting, perform a little research on Instagram to look what similar debts are doing and their target market's response. Since you could percentage comparable audiences, that is a superb way to determine out what works and what does not. It additionally allows you find out capability producers you would probably paintings with as quickly as your emblem is mounted in case you're an influencer. At this component, you want to discover famous money owed and the extremely good hashtags on Instagram for your content material fabric. You also can use a internet web page like numerous-hashtags.Com to find out the exceptional hashtags to your hassle count wide variety. For example, I typed "Leadership" on the web net page and were given 30 of the quality hashtags.

Influencer tip:

If you realize a specific brand you want to work with similarly down the road, studies the influencers they currently use. Follow those influencers and word the campaigns they create, the hashtags, and the sort of content fabric they positioned out. Learn as an awful lot as you could and do your excellent to create content fabric cloth geared in the direction of that brand's hobbies and assignment.

Step #three: Find the gaps

The subsequent vital step as you waft towards defining your location of hobby is to discover gaps that you can fill in terms of content material fabric. Is there a topic you experience wants to get the eye it merits? For example, in case you need a vegan recipe account, you could recognition greater on natural cruelty-free products due to the truth no person is doing that. That may be a superb manner to create a name for yourself interior a broader magnificence.

Step #4: Research what your perfect goal market cares about

Remember that listing of passions, skills, and skills? It's time to healthful it up with an goal marketplace. This will assist you shortlist the wonderful area of interest quicker than any other step. It's additionally one of the most important steps you can take because it focuses on serving your destiny target audience. Of path, if you have no goal market or patron base, this workout may require more research and some gut steerage. What it comes all of the way proper all the way down to is answering some questions. Namely:

What trouble or assignment is my first-rate customer facing?

What choice or aspiration does my best client have?

What values do we percentage in common?

What type of content do they maximum care about?

Chapter 10: Do You Know Your Ideal Audience?

You've in all likelihood heard that Instagram is one of the maximum famous social networks inside the international. It's ranked 6th inside the worldwide, with 1 billion customers outstanding handed by means of Facebook (2.6 billion), YouTube (2.0 billion), WhatsApp (1.6 billion), Messenger 1.Three billion), and WeChat (1.1 billion). The exceptional element is that Instagram has a full-size worldwide goal market. But having an worldwide target market technique you could serve only a few humans at the platform. So in advance than starting our content material approach for Instagram, we want to investigate the conduct of the customers to discern out what your perfect target audience loves to revel in at the platform virtually so your content material material can bypass in that course. You have selected your place of hobby and already recognize what troubles, aspirations, and topics your target audience well-knownshows thrilling, but how do you align that with content material introduction? By moving into the thoughts of your exceptional fan. First, on the same time as surfing the platform, You should recognize who they'll be and their intellectual u.S.A. Of america.

Instagram Users Statistics You Should Know

We all behave and set unique expectancies for the severa systems we draw close out on. MY MINDSET IS DIFFERENT after I am on YouTube than when I am on TikTok or Instagram. The equal is real to your high-quality target marketplace, so it's far critical to apprehend how customers behave on Instagram and what content cloth is maximum attractive to them.

Here are some precious stats which you need to apprehend from 2020.

Five hundred million each day lively clients are gaining access to the app globally.

People spend a mean of 28 minutes a day at the Instagram app. Users under 25 spend even greater time at the app, with records showing the younger demographic spending 32 minutes while the ones over 25 spend 24 mins.

The most popular global places with the super usage consist of the us (a hundred and twenty million), India (eighty million), Brazil (seventy seven million), Indonesia (sixty three million), and Russia (forty four million). Five hundred million each day energetic customers are getting access to the app globally.

22.02% of the arena's 4.Fifty 4 billion lively Internet clients access Instagram monthly.

In the united states, 75% of people elderly 18 - 24 use Instagram, positioned with the useful resource of fifty seven% among 25 - 30 years vintage.

Globally, gender use is quite even, with 50.Nine% female and 49.1% male customers.

In the usa, adult clients are forty three% ladies and 31% guys.

Brands typically appearance to producers with 50,000 to one hundred,000 fans to promote their products. This significant range, however, may be an awful lot tons much less relying on area of hobby and enterprise.

According to the 2020 records, the first-class time to place up on Instagram is among 10:00 pm and 2:pm Central Daylight Time. The exceptional days are Wednesday at eleven:00 a.M. And Friday among 10:00 a.M. To eleven:00 a.M.

Instagram photographs get an average of 23% more engagement than Facebook.

Posts with movement pictures get preserve of 38% extra engagement than pictures.

70% of customers look up manufacturers on Instagram.

79% of clients are looking for for Instagram for records on a services or products.

80% of clients take a look at at the least one logo on Instagram.

One-1/3 of Instagram clients have purchased via the platform on cellular.

70% of clients need to look manufacturers they opt for and observe taking a stand on social issues that count range to them. Of the ones, sixty 5% need the brands to take that stand on social media.

The common engagement rate for branded posts is 4.Three%.

Having as a minimum one hashtag can boom engagement by means of as a good deal as 12.6%.

Longer hashtags get extra results. The debate stays on, but the magic quantity is eleven hashtags for each located up in case you need most amazing outcomes.

Four hundred million customers watch Instagram Stories every day.

forty six% of Instagram Stories clients like humorous and unique content material cloth.

Brand Stories have an 85% final touch fee.

Should You Pay Attention And Leverage Your Instagram Competitors?

The smooth solution is positive and no. If you've got the right goal and technique, these debts can end up a fantastic supply of information, thought, and lead era. No, if you're from a loss of mentality and excellent want to duplicate others.

Instagram has plenty of human beings to reveal into followers, so that you should in no manner enjoy intimidated by means of the use of using the reality that you could find out influencers and profile money owed already set up in your selected vicinity of interest. I encourage you to look this as an amazing trouble. Think approximately it. Finding an account with an already set up target market of mother and father that would moreover benefit from your content makes it less tough on the way to make bigger your account as long as you do it the ethical manner.

You can broaden your Instagram account through networking, following, attractive with, and setting up relationships with influencers on your region. Find authority content cloth and select out the most crucial statements that resonate with you and show signs of an engaged goal marketplace. I propose developing a listing of 10 expenses and analyzing the subsequent:

What is their follower do not forget?

How often do they publish?

What engagement do they get on common?

What scenario are you able to come to be privy to from their feed?

How frequently do they placed up Instagram Stories and IGTV?

What hashtags are they the use of the maximum? What's the big variety do not forget of hashtags used on every positioned up?

What is their branding like? For example, have a take a look at their tone of voice, shades, fonts, filters, messaging, and so forth.

What do they select posting about? Are there any gaps within the sort of content material they're posting that you can post for your feed?

The motive of your competitor evaluation is to have a look at as a bargain as you may out of your competition so you can installation the following guidelines.

#1. Consider doing an outreach advertising and marketing marketing campaign to all the money owed that resonate with you and suggest a collaboration.

#2. Comment, like, percentage, store, repost, comply with, or perhaps create content citing the content material material material you want from a competitor. Then tag them. And while you comment on a image or video, make it considerate and treasured to the community so unique clients can also enjoy your persona.

#3. Consider offering to manage their account completely free so that you can sell your content material. The owner will possibly take transport of your thought in case you choose an appropriate statements with a extremely good following, immoderate engagement, and no corresponding weblog or website. Although this method will contain extra attempt, it moreover opens you as a tremendous deal as an already set up goal market, that means you can exponentially boom your following interior days or weeks.

#4. If you run a few paid advertisements, I encourage you to find out a competitor with a healthy target audience period and run commercials in opposition to them. If you use this technique, polish up your Instagram profile and bio to create resonance in case you need to straight away experience a connection with you. For instance, if the competitor is close by, consider which includes your town call to your profile.

Bonus tip:

If you need to dig your heels in with an natural technique that does not rate a dime, right right here's an amazing hack. Follow one hundred of your pinnacle opposition' lovers. After you look at a person, browse via their feed and locate among one and three posts you may observe and touch upon. Make that remark thoughtful, and do not be afraid to use a few emojis and your specific persona. It will take some earlier investment of time and electricity, however I can assure you at the least a 34% follow-up end result absolutely through utilizing this simple hack.

Targeting Your Audience

Everything hinges on our capability to determine who your content material might be created for accurately. Suppose we want to beautify on producing content material material that engages a specific enterprise employer of human beings from the one billion Instagram users. In that case, monetizing your account could be next to now not possible. The records I definitely have shared on this monetary catastrophe display that many energetic users are already setting out at the platform every day. Unfortunately, they may notwithstanding the reality that have interaction with and purchase out of your emblem. So, how do we play to make certain the possibilities are for your need? By making an funding a ton of time defining your intention marketplace and generally sporting out checks to have a look at extra about your tribe.

The first element you have to do is put in force confirmed strategies that get this accomplished. Suppose you need an cutting-edge patron base, commercial enterprise information to move with the resource of, or enthusiasts from other social media structures to leverage; what then?

Start wherein you are with what you comprehend. Ask your self the subsequent questions:

Who is my services or products designed for?

What is my best target market searching out?

What verbal exchange is taking place on my competitor's account that could supply me a glimpse of what my fine target marketplace wishes extra?

Use a tool like Phalanx Influencer Auditor to provide you with insights which consist of demographics, logo mentions, follower locations, and engagement levels. That will enable you to see missing goal market segments you continue to need to seize up on, the form of content fabric cloth your human beings can also like, and the most energetic follower locations for your services or products.

The subsequent component you want to do is display your Instagram analytics as you positioned up and have interaction on the facet of your community. Instagram can inform you plenty about your target market, specifically when you have a commercial corporation account. If you want to learn how to switch to a industrial corporation account, I will show off it in an upcoming phase. Once you have got were given been running beneath the proper form of account for some time, records will populate your Instagram insights, which may be accessed through going to the "Insights" tab > "Audience." You'll studies extra approximately your existing lovers and their area, gender, age range, and so forth. Add this statistics to the file you have got been filling in so far, and you can have a healthy records of what your aim marketplace looks as if.

Once you have got an concept of your target marketplace, it is time to acquire out. All the records you've got amassed will simplest imply a issue if you located it to suited use via growing content material specific to that individual organization and appealing them within the community. For example, you may begin with the aid of the use of the use of figuring out those warm hashtags your perfect goal marketplace often makes use of. These hashtags have to be blanketed for your submit in which appropriate. You need to moreover make investments a while every day clicking on the ones hashtags to find pinnacle-performing content material so that you can commentary, like, and interact with others who've commented. Get your voice heard and percent your opinion wherein you find today's conversations for your area of interest. That let you get determined through the use of all the right humans. A neat trick is to join a social listening tool that allows you to obtain notifications of topics getting pretty some attention on social media.

Another element you may do is hook up with the proper influencers to your area. Create impossible to face up to incentives for the influencers that serve your high-quality goal market. You can find out the ones influencers thru hashtag research, as said earlier than, or through the usage of systems like Influencer. Co. The exceptional manner this can yield powerful consequences is if you plan on the offer for the partnership. Do you've got a notable services or products you could supply out for the influencer to take a look at? Can you partner up for a giveaway contest or have them do a take-over of your Instagram for a tough and fast duration? You want to parent out what's going to be attractive to the influencer. When starting, stick with micro-influencers, as they'll possibly discover your offer valuable. They are also less difficult to attain.

Chapter 11: Branding Your Instagram Account

If you do not have an Instagram account, now will be the time to do it. I will walk you thru the easy approach, and you could usually reference the Instagram assist middle for any snags or new updates. Even when you have an Instagram account, I suggest going via this entire economic break. You can continuously select out up tricks and ideas at the manner to decorate.

Creating An Account

The first detail you want to do is download the app from the App Store or Google Play Store, depending for your telephone. Once set up, tap the Instagram icon to open and click on the "Sign Up"/ "Create Account" button to create a new account. Use your email cope with or phone quantity and faucet "Next." If you pick the use of Facebook, then you definately definately have the choice to join up in conjunction with your Facebook account. You'll then be brought about to log into your Facebook account in case you're currently logged out. If you sign on with an e mail or cellphone range, create a username and password, fill out your profile information, and tap Next.

The default putting for all Instagram customers is a non-public account. We want to use it to construct our emblem and market our business enterprise, so we should switch it to a business enterprise account and be part of it to a Facebook industrial corporation net page. To link for your Facebook money owed and percent posts right away from Instagram to Facebook, you want to visit your profile and faucet the menu icon. Then click on the little cogwheel for "Settings" > "Account" > Linked Accounts > Facebook. Enter your Facebook Login facts and choose out the web page you want to be associated with this account.

If you're questioning the way to transfer from a non-public account to a business organisation account, it's super easy. Go to your profile and faucet the menu in the higher right nook. Then visit "Settings" > "Account" > "Switch to Professional Account" > "Business." Here, you need to feature records together with industrial business enterprise elegance (which need to be chosen based totally definitely totally on your location of interest) and call information. Once statistics is stuffed in, then faucet "Done."

Personal Versus Business Account

Do you understand the distinction between a private and industrial company account, or why we insist on switching to a commercial enterprise organization account?

Let's start with the fact that handiest with a commercial organisation account will you be able to build up analytics from Instagram telling you more about your audience. That will permit you to recognise which posts are acting high-quality, which viewers got here through your preferred hashtags, and the manner a number of the money owed being reached are currently following you. You can also get insights into your target market demographics.

A enterprise account will provide you with get right of entry to to lots more top elegance capabilities, collectively with the capability to feature the "swipe up" feature after you get to ten,000 or more lovers, and you additionally get a "contact" button in order that people can name or email you without delay from Instagram. With the release of the Instagram keep and Reels, having a business organization account has in no way been more important because handiest with a business enterprise account do you get the chance to show up at the Explore net page thru your reels. And, of path, having an in-built Instagram store makes it smooth for a follower to buy some element from you.

Tips For Setting Up Your Profile

Anyone can set up an Instagram profile inside a couple of minutes, however placing one up that draws new fans requires loads of careful

171

attention. I am sharing quality practices for successfully putting in place your Instagram profile.

Tip #1: Make extremely good you've switched to a employer profile

We've already referred to the advantages of putting in your account as a commercial company profile. You want every body global to view your extremely good feed and your posts to have a much wider acquire so anybody who resonates collectively together with your profile can immediately follow you. This is some of the maximum critical subjects you could do while putting in location your profile.

Tip #2: Use the proper photo that authentically expresses you and your brand

If your emblem is targeted spherical you, i.E., a private brand, I encourage you to use an accurate picture of yourself. Look at money owed which include Marie Forleo, Gary Vaynerchuck, and Tai Lopez for super examples of normal parents who've constructed a success Instagram payments. More people resonate with them because of the truth they encounter as approachable and right. You want the identical notion collectively together with your logo. However, in case you select the organisation direction, examine from money owed together with Hubspot, Buffer, and CoSchedule. Use a clean logo and make certain it aligns together together with your essential net internet site and the emblem identity. You might in all likelihood regulate your primary emblem to healthy better with the platform's dimensions but maintain the genuine look consistent.

Tip #3: Choose the first-rate username and Instagram name

Picking a call it is memorable, searchable, and aligns at the side of your logo identification is extra hard than one would possibly probably assume. Be aware of the phrase you agree for, specially in case you're going for a username one of a type from your real name or organisation name.

You have as much as thirty characters for your cope with; no symbols or areas want to exist. This is the selection people will use when they aspect out you in a remark or within the event that they want to tag you in some factor, so select out out correctly. If you can't discover some factor clean and innovative, you can commonly use your call in preference to combining it collectively along with your sturdy point, e.G., Suzie, who focuses on vegan cuisine recipes, can name herself Suze_veganlife or Vegan_Suzie. To edit your @username, go to the profile web page > "Edit Profile." Click at the text or vicinity next to the person icon and enter the favored username.

You can exchange the Instagram call as regularly as you need to test out special titles that speak what your target market will resonate with. However, I do not advise frequently changing your username because of the reality you may want to alternate all the places you introduced or linked to this username. Otherwise, people receives a "broken link" or mistakes page once they click on on your vintage hyperlinks.

Tip #four: Make your bio informative and appealing

Your bio on Instagram is the define at the top of your profile. It's what new site visitors will see once they first come upon your profile. Depending on the number one effect that your phrases make, a person is more likely to browse through your feed, engage alongside aspect your account, and in the long run examine you, or they may click on away. The reproduction in this bio is, therefore, crucial. You handiest have 100 and fifty characters to tell people what you're approximately and why they ought to comply with you. That's a piece location to particular yourself completely, so you need pretty some creativity to make this paintings.

The amazing way to approach this is to assume from the angle of your capacity follower. They land for your profile both due to the truth they observed your located up thru a hashtag they look at or a few wonderful cause. What need to your bio profile say to make this character more inquisitive about adding you to their feed? What's in it for them? Why must they care about your account? How will you beautify their international and cause them to experience better?

As you provide you together with your thoughts, do not be afraid to add your character and play around with applicable emojis so people can "experience" the tone of your brand identity. An example I like is from Oreo's Instagram account. On their profile, they write, " See the area through our OREO Wonderfilled lens." You can also check out Nike. They frequently tweak their bio, but I specifically like " Spotlighting athlete and ��� (Sport shoe icon) memories."

Tip #5: Make the maximum of your clickable hyperlink.

You've were given one hazard to direct humans in your net internet site or offer, so save the link on your bio. That hyperlink is one of the maximum valuable real belongings areas for using net website online traffic in your precise products or services. To keep subjects amazing clean, you could use a trendy link from your touchdown internet web page and frequently update it with the state-of-the-art gives. Savvy Instagrammers use equipment like Tailwind to take subjects further and create a connection with more than one gadgets. Regardless of your choice, track that link to advantage records approximately the customers clicking to analyze greater about your brand.

Tip #6: Create an attractive grid to your feed

Why is this critical? Well, consider it. When we find out a state-of-the-art account, we test out the profile percent bio and instantly scroll all of the manner all the way down to browse the feed. If our eyes and emotions resonate with what we see, it's an right now enchantment, and we're in all likelihood to interact with and look at that account. If the feed repels us, it might not depend number how an awful lot we liked the profile p.C and bio; we are able to in all likelihood click on on away with out turning into lovers.

I in reality have frequently encountered a submit at the same time as surfing a hashtag that topics to me and clicked thru to test out greater from the account. Once there, I emerge as disinterested inside the statistics because of the truth the relaxation of the feed goals to talk to me. Most Instagrammers want to apprehend what number of lovers they'll lose because of the fact they want to invest time questioning via their grid layout.

It's nearly like cooking and serving the fantastic materials on an unappetizing plate. No one will need to devour that meals. So, take into account this exercising as essential as growing great content material cloth and writing accurate replica to your bio. To make sure you put yourself up for fulfillment, craft a sample following the prevailing rows of threes that Instagram offers. Your content can repeat in multiples of 3, six, 9, twelve, or whatever you need, and it's going to constantly appear like there's an overarching pattern that allows you to create a revel in of symmetry and consistency. For instance, I've observed this pattern on one in every of my Instagram money owed through switching amongst white and coloured backgrounds. So, submit #1 is a white records, post #2 is a coloured historic past, located up #3 is a white statistics, submit #four is a white historic past, submit #five is a colored records, and so on. You also can pass a distinct direction if you promote a particular product with the useful resource of making every 1/3 positioned up an photo of that product. For instance, if you promote pup accessories, every zero.33 put up is probably an accessory. That may additionally in the end create that enjoy of consistency for your grid.

Advanced tip:

If you are comfortable with coloration coordination, use shade scheme coordination with the resource of using pairing comparable tones and colorings in your grid. Just make certain the transition is seamless. It's pleasant for feeds focusing more on selfies and human pictures due to the fact the precept problem.

How To Brand On Instagram

Branding is a massive subject matter, so we're able to attention at the primary technical things you need to understand and put in force for our amateur's adventure. After all, it'll take quite some art work to stand out within the ocean of fellow Instagrammers if human beings cannot right away understand what you stand for and what makes you specific. So, at the same time as you take into account branding, technique it from the viewpoint of evoking a specific emotion and notion. It's about growing an revel in on your fans and capability enthusiasts. So, what experience do you want to have, and the manner do you want people to preserve in thoughts you? Are you fun? Clean and minimalist? Youthful and rebellious? Serious and formal?

Branding is all about storytelling, accept as true with-building, and belief. It want to be well timed, and it will take time to appear. Every post moves you alongside this adventure, so that you need to make clear your imaginative and prescient on your Instagram net web page and the project or motive for growing it. Always anchor your self in those vital foundational elements as making a decision what brand you are building. Another aspect you want to reflect onconsideration on is the tonality and persona which you want people to revel in. A comical feed and a extreme or impersonal tone might be awkward. That loss of congruency for your branding would in all likelihood unconsciously throw human beings off. The equal is actual for the colors and fonts.

The colorings, font, and imagery you operate have to paint this image to a person in seconds. Most human beings start this adventure of branding with the beneficial useful resource of developing a temper board. You can do this on software program application like InVision without charge.

The subsequent issue you want is to decide on logo sun shades. Instagram is a one hundred% seen-primarily based app emphasizing aesthetics, so have fun proper right here. Be real to your self and find out shade mixtures that let you precise who you're while ultimate relevant for your brand's message and provide. Different colorings and shades have a taken into consideration one of a type impact on the customer. Some are perceived as calming or younger, at the equal time as others appear bold, rebellious, or gothic. This step may additionally take everywhere from a couple of hours to severa days. But strive no longer to overthink it. A beneficial useful useful resource that may guide you in selecting the proper colour for your Instagram emblem is Colors. Cafe. They clearly have an inspiring Instagram account that posts colour palettes with each shade code listed to hurry up your choice-making manner. You can also test out Pantone on Instagram, in which they percentage many extremely good thoughts on mixing and matching shades.

Once you have determined on a colour, it is time to discover an appropriate font. Although the captions use a current font on Instagram, your posts will require textual content sometimes until you most effective cognizance on selfies. This a part of your branding is essential for a motivational account with fees. The font you operate immediately tells a tale and well-knownshows your personality. One issue I want to detail out in advance than encouraging you to choose out out a font is to keep in thoughts of the font kind because of the truth at the same time as some are incredibly lovable, they'll be difficult to look or have a study at the Instagram feed. This is a cell-first app, so the whole thing wants to be ideal for the small display show.

Serif, Sans serif, Display, and Modern are the first-class and most effective to check on mobile. Serif fonts supposedly represent way of life, respectability, and discernment. San serifs are current, goal, present day, and related to innovation. Current fonts are taken into consideration stylish and sturdy. Display fonts are often related to friendliness, entertainment, and expressiveness. To assist you make a decision out what fonts you want to use, don't forget the use of a layout app like Canva, which has an top notch font library to play with. They sincerely have prepared-made templates and font pairings. You also can comply with the "We Love Branding" Instagram account for idea.